The Roadmap to Finding Your Passion
and the Courage to Pursue It

YOUR TIME IS NOW

TAMMY L. BREZNITSKY

YOUR TIME IS NOW
The Roadmap to Finding Your Passion and the Courage to Pursue It

Difference Press, Washington, D.C., USA
© Tammy L. Breznitsky, 2021

ISBN: 978-1-68309-296-4

No part of this publication in any form should be considered medical advice.

Neither the author nor the publisher assumes any responsibility for errors, omissions, or contrary interpretations of the subject matter herein. Any perceived slight of any individual or organization is purely unintentional.

Brand and product names are trademarks or registered trademarks of their respective owners.

Cover Design: Jennifer Stimson
Interior Book Design: Kozakura
Editing: Emily Tuttle
Author's photo courtesy of: Ian Jansen

For Sam — you are and forever will be my guide, my truth, my fear slayer, my heart, my ever-present connection to that which is real, and a constant reminder this is so.

TABLE OF CONTENTS

CHAPTER 1

THE GOLDEN HANDCUFFS

"There is no intermediate step between ice and water, but there is one between life and death: employment."
— Nassim Nicholas Taleb

You likely know this scenario: you are called into the big fancy corner office. There is a man behind a big desk; he's likely white, in his fifties, and balding. He leans back and asks, "So, tell me, where do you see yourself in this organization in five years?"

Oh, the infamous question. But it's also my favorite question because the answer is easy when you have big plans for your career. Well, at least that's the part I verbalized to my boss. What I was really thinking at that moment was, "Five years? Uh, yeah ... so I've been up since 3:00 a.m. with a sick baby and I'm pretty sure I now have a fever too. So frankly, I'm just trying to get through the next seven hours of this freaking interview without barfing, thanks so much."

But of course, I didn't say that.

I showed up as exactly who I was at that time – the strong, vibrant, hard-working, disciplined, kick-butt, hard-headed, always-pull-through-regardless-of-the-number-of-hours-of-sleep-she-got-with-or-without-a-fever Tammy. So I answered with exactly what I believed to be true: "In five years, I'll be an executive director of the HCV field team. I will not be leading just *any* field team, I will build and lead *the best field team our investigators have ever worked with and this company has ever employed.*"

I made a decision a long time ago that there was nothing that could get in the way of my dream of being an influential woman and leader of medical affairs in the pharmaceutical industry. It was going to be me sitting behind that corner desk, and I was going to get there with grit and grace. I was going to empower and inspire women leaders across the industry. So, having a baby with a fever and interviewing for a job on little or no sleep was a no-brainer – really, it was a piece of cake compared to what I lived through to get to that point in my life and career. Although I admit that being a working mother posed a new and different kind of challenge to me at that time, it was one that I most certainly wasn't going to let stop me.

Sounds pretty driven and bold, right?

I will tell you this much right off the bat – that interview took place over ten years ago. I am not an executive director (ED) or a senior vice president (SVP).

I am the CEO of my life and I have big magic to work on this earth.

Guess what? You do too.

Ok, so now you are likely asking, "Wait, what? Did I pick up the right book?"

Yes, of course you did. Actually, this book more than likely found *you*.

I'm going to take a guess and bet you too are incredibly successful. I'm going to bet if you aren't successful right now, you are on your way there, right? Maybe someone has dubbed you a "rising star." Maybe you have been given numerous opportunities to attend leadership trainings or programs since you have "high potential." You might even be running those leadership programs. Maybe you are the SVP, being groomed for CEO. The point is that you have big dreams, don't you? You can see yourself behind that desk or on that stage. You are a natural-born leader, and you too love responding to that question, "Where will you be in five years?" because you always know the answer.

I'm also going to bet that you work your behind off. Maybe someone gave you a good start to your life and career, or maybe, like me, it took a whole lot of blood, sweat, and tears to get here. If your case is the latter, then your work means a lot to you, doesn't it? Either way, you work hard every day, and all of this hard work likely has taught you how to thrive in challenge. Well, let's be honest, what corporate work environment today isn't challenging? But the challenge most days keeps you spry and on your toes, and you are learning to navigate all the politics and drama like a ninja. In fact, you don't just like a challenge – you look for them, ask to be involved, speak up where you can to add value, and when you agree to take on that challenge, you give 110 percent. You do so because you care, you know hard work pays off, and you know it will give you the exposure you need to get to where you are going, right?

It's the joy of the chase, of the next rung on the ladder.

I loved the chase. I lived for it. I remember always being on the lookout for the next "dumpster fire" I could take on or the next project I could become involved in. I believed I needed "that" job or to become involved in "that" project because I believed I could do it better, get noticed, and be considered for the next opportunity to lead, which would move me up that ladder. I became caught up in the seemingly never-ending chase to prove who I was, what kind of leader I could be, and how I could perform and deliver under pressure while being professional, politically correct, polished, calm, and collected. And as a woman, I could do it all with sick babies, no sleep, and a fever, with thoughts about what I needed to stop and get on the way home to make for dinner running in the background.

I know how hard you work. I know how long your hours really are. I know what your Saturdays "off" look like.

I know you.

I see you.

And I want you to know that you are freaking amazing.

I mean it. Take a minute and think about how amazing you really are.

There is nothing more to say than that I honor you, and I know the work you put in to get here and the things you have to juggle every day to show up the way you do. So, everything you have, you deserve to have. You own it. As you should.

As did I.

From early in my career, I was told I was talented enough that I could do it all and have it all, and I did a good job creating a lifestyle that represented exactly that. I worked in pharmacy as an infectious diseases clinical pharmacy specialist, began speaking for various companies, and ultimately made a jump to industry within a few years. My career ladder looked like this: medical science liaison (MSL) to senior MSL to associate field team director to associate global strategy director to global strategy director to director of field strategy and training. Not too long ago, I had an opportunity to apply for that ED role I declared I wanted a decade ago, which I didn't go after.

More on that later, but the bottom line is that I was enjoying a pretty successful career, and the future was bright. I was traveling the world, working hard, and I'd like to believe I did so with grace and ease. I saw myself in that corner office. I have a wonderful husband who is and has always been incredibly supportive of my dreams, and together, we are proud of the life we have created. I am proud of my story and how I chose to rise from the circumstances of my life that were less than desirable. I did what I promised myself I would do, and I was on the trajectory to the kind of executive-level success I dreamed of having.

One day, I was in my business class seat on another flight abroad, going through my usual routine. I swallowed down my Ativan with a glass of champagne so I could sleep on the way to Heathrow in order to go right into a meeting once we landed. As I got out my pill bottle, I heard a gentle whisper in my heart, *"How long are we going to do this?"*

It stopped me in my tracks.

I quickly thought, "Stop. Of course I am hearing this. I am tired. Of course I feel sad. I am leaving my family again. But this is what successful people do. They are tired and sad, but they fight through it. They take anti-anxiety pills and champagne when they have to. This is what it takes, and this is the cost. Everything comes with a cost, and I manage it well."

The voice fell silent.

Time carried on as it does, with one meeting after another. I planned my days and weeks and months until, like some unexpected surprise, Christmas would come back around again. I can say that I actually started to hate Christmas. It felt like so much work to me – decorating, cleaning, cooking, shopping. Bleh.

Of course I always rose to the occasion, year after year. I smiled through it, did what I needed to do, and everything always got done. My husband is a rock star and my children are gems who always gave me the boost I needed to get back into the spirit of the holidays, but generally, they would have to drag me along for a good while. That feeling of being tired and dragged along when you are supposed to feel happy is a cue, isn't it? But I found it was easier to just push it away, and even easier to justify it. "Of course you are tired, Tammy, look what you do every day!" So I began to see my busy travel schedule as representative of my success, and I wore my tiredness like a badge of honor. Life seemed to be speeding by as the seasons seemed to change, sometimes without my awareness. "Oh wow, it's Easter next week!" But I just kept going, because I felt it was just, well, how life goes.

I was living in this continuous cycle of work, travel, kids' activities, and holidays, trying to fit in working out, coupling it with drinking and friends and more drinking and recovering in between, all so I could go back to work "refreshed" from the weekend. At one point in my career, I began to realize that on vacation, I would begin to feel sadness rear its head mid-week regardless of where we were because that meant I only had a few more days with my family before going back to work. I found I was really bumming after a three-day weekend. The bottom line is that I realized I was no longer looking forward to work. I was sad I had work the next day and many days, and if I was traveling that coming week, I absolutely dreaded it.

Sound familiar? If so, maybe these thoughts, which I had in my head at various points in my career, will resonate with you too:

7

- How is it that I can be working so hard, but at the same time still feel like it's not enough? The next rung on the ladder requires even more of me. How much harder can I really work? What am I doing this for?

- Why do others in other positions seem so happy and I'm not?

- How can I have so much, but find it hard to enjoy what I have? Why does it feel so empty and temporary? Why do I feel empty?

- How can I make my work more meaningful? What am I really killing myself for? What am I getting out of it? Is this really all there is?

- Is my success screwing up my kids? Will they look back and wish they had more of me? Am I failing them?

- How can I continue to maintain my relationship with my husband when I'm never home? Does he even care? Does he notice how hard I'm working? Does he see how much I do for him and this family? Does it matter?

If we are really being honest here, maybe you have heard yourself thinking other things like this:

- I'm so out of shape. I gained weight because all I do is sit at this desk, in this chair, and on this phone, mostly dealing with other people's problems, and then I come home to a crazy house with screaming kids and a husband caught up in his own work. So I drink and eat it all away at night. Something has got to give.

- That's it. It's Saturday – on Monday, I am going to eat well and try to work out regularly. But then Thursday at 6 a.m. – who am I kidding? I don't have time for this. I'm so freaking tired, and I have that meeting I have to prepare for.

- Look at those bags under my eyes and the dimples on my legs... pathetic.

- Oh wait, that weekend is the soccer tournament... Ugh... Looks like I'll be making slides during the game.

- I just need a drink. A few glasses of wine and everything will be tolerable again.

- Maybe my marriage isn't what I thought? Maybe I need to find someone who gets me in a different way.

- My kids are entitled little brats who don't want for anything, but it's still not enough. I don't know what to do with them already. They are never happy.

Tough stuff to read, but it's real. You know it.

If you are like me, you too likely have always been in touch with yourself enough to know what feels right and what doesn't. I knew that this wasn't how I wanted to feel about my life. I wanted to feel alive. I wanted to wake up excited about work. Most importantly, I wanted to do something that made a difference, and I was seeing more clearly that those fleeting moments of perceived happiness I was enjoying in this career were temporary and superficial. I knew I needed to do something, but I had no idea what. So I did the only thing I knew how to – I kept moving forward trusting I would eventually figure it out.

The ironic thing is how much easier it is to do this when you are paid well to be miserable. Money is such a sly manipulator because it shows up so readily as the great equalizer, but when I began to see through it, I realized that all it really offers is the illusion of safety with a dose here and there of fleeting happiness – just enough to keep those golden handcuffs tight and secured.

Yes, I felt "financially secure," and I was generally "happy" and grateful for what I was doing, including the privileges I enjoyed because of my hard work, but deep inside my heart, I knew I was unsettled. At night, I would lay in bed and my head would be spinning. I was doing everything right, but I still was feeling like there had to be more. *This couldn't be it.*

Then I would scold myself. "Tammy, you work hard, and you deserve what you have. Be grateful for all of it. Be present. What you want and need to make a difference is waiting at the next level, and you are on your way. That what's wrong. More is coming. Just lean in."

So I did because it's what we do, right? We lean in.

The joy of the chase.

I worked harder, and of course, to compensate, I bought more things for myself. I'm thinking this is familiar to you too because leaning in has to be counterbalanced with something on the other side, or we would all go bonkers. Isn't it interesting that high-profile executive positions are generally tied to a very good salary, which nicely allows for this to be the case?

The truth is that corporate America creates this title-work-money story for us that we buy into like Pavlovian dogs – titles mean more prestige and influence, which means more money, which clearly means access to more things that will make us happy (in theory). So we keep going and working ourselves to death, believing we will be happy when we can take the next big trip, buy our dream car, hire a manicurist, get regular massages, maybe hire a nutritionist to eat well, or a personal trainer to keep us fit. But at the end of the day, this will ultimately become an added stressor because we will have to fight with ourselves to make time for it, because fitting these things in is just one more thing to do, and it feels horrible because we are exhausted.

We hire nannies and babysitters who drive and can be present for our kids because we can't, all for the sake of leaning in. I would claim that my children and family were always my highest priority, and although I made every effort to *physically* be there, which made me feel better, I'm not sure I was actually *present*. I had conference calls and slides to make. I had presentations to practice. "Ok, honey, I just have one more thing and then I'm closing down. I promise." I can hear myself saying it as I type it.

Believe me, I leaned and leaned and leaned and leaned. I bet you do too.

I found leaning in more only got me two things: more responsibility and more exhaustion. I actually had less energy, was more grouchy, yelled more at my kids, became easily annoyed with my husband, and in general, had a very low threshold for people who weren't living up to my standards of hard work and success. It all made me feel alienated, frustrated, and angry at home and at work, and when you feel that way, everything else looks that way too. I think this is where confusion and anger really take root because, regardless of what you have and can buy in the material world, you are still empty inside and feel like you are running on empty, which only creates more frustration and more confusion.

Here is what I'm here to tell you today: while you are busy leaning in, feeling exhausted and run down, running meeting to meeting and airplane to airplane, and working through the seemingly endless planning and coordination that is your life, *precious time and the real magic of life is slipping away right before your eyes.*

Remember in the beginning of this chapter, I mentioned this book found you? Here's why: because what you think you want isn't really what you need. You don't need another promotion. You don't need another vacation. You don't need to buy anything else or get another massage or have another drink.

What if I told you that your discontentment with your life right now is there for a reason? That feeling restless is only the trigger for you to begin an incredible journey to something more wonderful than you could ever imagine? What if at the end of that journey, you found that you had something very special you were being called to do, something that the world needs and that only you can give? What if I told you that this book can help you not only uncover what that thing is, but can help you know exactly what you should do next? In fact, I can promise that what will be revealed to you at the end of this journey will be so perfect for you that you will come to understand that it was yours all along. It will change you forever, set your life on fire, and you will feel more alive than ever before. You will beam light from inside of you. People will ask you what has changed, what you are doing differently, and say that they want what you are having. The best part? You already have everything you need. The only thing you need to do is show up exactly as you are with an open heart and open mind ready to do the work.

How do I know?

Because I found my way. You are reading this, aren't you?

It really is quite simple.

The answers you are looking for are inside of you.

How to get to those answers is in the book in your hand.

CHAPTER 2

THE JOURNEY TO THE KEY

"I believe in the sun even when it is not shining, I believe in love even when I cannot feel it, I believe in God even when he is silent."
– written on a cellar wall by a prisoner of the Holocaust

AN AFTERNOON WALK

I grew up in a small coal-mining town in Schuylkill County Pennsylvania called Mahanoy City. I didn't know it at the time, but we really were living in quintessential small-town America, composed of a melting pot of cultural influences of mostly Eastern Europeans whose families moved there during the anthracite coal boom for steady work. It was notoriously known as the place where there was a church and a bar on every corner. Looking back, it was really much more than that. It was a place where people worked hard, drank too much to cope with the hard work, and gossiped about each other, but also took care of each other without blinking an eye. There was this unspoken loyalty that was never doubted or questioned. Throughout my childhood, so many different people influenced my life just because they "took care of me" in one way or another. I will never forget the kindness and love they showed to me. It formed me on many levels, and for that, I am forever grateful.

We lived in a half-double on Pine Street across from a larger set of row homes. I loved our little neighborhood. It was the kind of place where, in the summer, children left their houses in the morning after eating a bowl of cereal and watching Cartoon Express, went out to the park to meet friends, and only came home to eat or when the streetlights came on.

My first real spiritual experience happened in Mahanoy City outside of our little house. It was a bright, sunny day in early April, but there was a chill in the air from the lingering winter season. I was ten years old and outside in the alley by my house, seeing who was around to play as my mom suggested I should. I was wearing my pink spring jacket and, of course, a hat, gloves, and a scarf because, well, April in Northeastern Pennsylvania isn't exactly warm. In fact, I have many fond memories of wearing a beautiful Easter dress covered by a big bulky winter coat, matching hat, and gloves standing outside of church freezing my behind off while my mom and grandmother chatted up neighbors and friends about Easter egg hunts in snow boots.

This afternoon, I was tinkering around in the street, and I remember that I suddenly became "aware" of things around me: the brightness of the sun and my shadow on the ground, leaves or something circling in the wind by my feet. Seemingly all at once, the sun became very bright and I was overcome with an overwhelming sense of indescribable joy, happiness, and immense love. I knew this love like I had known it my whole life. I said, "Oh, hi!" realizing I didn't need to use words, only thoughts, as I kicked along a rock as I walked.

Love and I had a nice little chat like this was a normal thing. It was like taking a walk in the park with your best friend in the whole wide world. I wish I could explain to you what it was like, but I can't even write this without crying because that's how wonderful it was. It was easy and joyful, and although I was not given the gift of being able to remember everything we talked about, I was left with this: everything was going to be OK. I had a very special job on earth that I would know another time, and I was loved no matter what. Like, love-loved forever and ever and ever. That kind of love I don't have words for. I remember thinking, "Oh, how I love you too!" Then the feeling left me, and I was back on the street walking along. I skipped off like it was just any other day, happy and peaceful. But it was not any other day. It was the beginning of something very special. Something sacred. Of course I didn't understand that at the time. I just felt happy. The truth is that moment changed my life forever, and I had no idea how much it would carry me through the darkest days of what was to come.

THE GAMBLER

I was raised in a family that had its problems like any other. My father was not a bad guy, but he wasn't a good guy either. He was a conflicted soul who wanted to be good and do good, but his own emotional scars from his family carried him to a place where dealing with pain created a victim mentality. So, he coped by seeking out pleasure in various ways.

When I was a child, his favorite vice was gambling. Whatever the occasion, he always took out his losses on my mother and saved a little for me and my sister, so fear-based discipline was the norm for us, including "getting the strap" when we didn't fall in line. As a child, "vacations" were rare, but when we took them, we went to a place where there was a casino. Having Atlantic City only three hours away from where we lived made this our "favorite" place to visit. My mom would take us to the beach all day and he would be absent, in the casino playing. We'd go back to the hotel, red as lobsters (because who needs sunscreen?) to meet him and I remember always dreading it, because we never knew what we were going to get when we saw him. If he lost, we knew we were in for a tough night and he would usually fight with my mother until we finally packed up the car and drove home. In fact, we left most places with my dad fighting with either my mother or someone we met along the way who made him mad, usually for reasons that were apparent only to him. There was always a scene. Always.

We normalized the yelling and the hitting that was part of our lives and lived by the unspoken "just forget about it" rule. Bad things that happened were never addressed or brought up in any way, and if you did try to bring up a sensitive subject you needed to talk about, you would be told "forget about it," which meant we were moving on and forgiveness was expected in there somewhere.

I have always tried to figure out how my mother allowed herself, my sister, and me to suffer such abuse. I almost hated her for it. I hated that she let him talk to her that way. I hated that she let him spit in her face and call her stupid and ugly. I hated that she let him call me a slut and not defend me. I hated that she let him use me to monopolize my sister's basketball career without caring for her or me emotionally. How could she not see? How could she let it go on like this and let it go? Of course, at that time, I didn't understand the depth of the emotional scars she herself was carrying. He had damaged her so deeply mentally and emotionally that even if she did see what was going on, she had no idea what to do. She was terrified of what she could do if she got an idea, and so she chose to suffer alongside us. After years of therapy, I am more compassionate to her plight, but being a mother, in my gut, I admit I will never understand it, and that's OK. I don't love her any less. I know in my heart she did her best.

As for me, I made a decision that I would never let any man, or person for that matter, treat me that way, including him. By the time I entered high school, I decided I was getting out of there. I had no idea how, but it didn't matter. I just put my head down and focused on school. I studied hard and graduated with distinguished honors. I applied and was accepted to the Philadelphia College of Pharmacy and Science and decided it was where I was going, although I had no idea how I or my parents were going to pay for it. It didn't matter.

My first two years of college were quite a mess on many levels. I had a very steady boyfriend who was my best friend in the whole world. I knew that he and his family loved me and worried about me, and this carried me in many ways. Leaving them and my little town to venture out into the big world was scary, and frankly, I felt like I was thrown to the wolves. The truth was that I had no idea who I was without my boyfriend Mike, and I'd never dealt with any of the emotional trauma of the life I lived through at home.

During my second year of college, my mother ended up getting very sick, close to death, and I remember coming home every weekend to help take care of my sister and things around the house. During my mother's illness, my dad's victim mentality went into overdrive. He could not understand why no one came to help him, so he basically cursed everyone, and I just assumed the role of taking care of him and my sister. I think he pretty much succumbed to the fact my mother was going to die and there is a part of me, in retrospect, that believes he had his eye on some insurance or a lawsuit for her death due to malpractice (which he actually did file eventually).

I remember coming home one weekend and going to see my mom. The doctor asked to speak to me privately and shared that my mom was very sick, likely going to die, and I should start to prepare myself. Being in pharmacy school, I had already started to read into what was going on with her care. I read her chart, looked up the terms, and was smart enough to figure it out. She had a burst gallbladder resulting in infection throughout her abdomen because someone missed the fact that the contents of her gallbladder were leaking into her peritoneal space.

I'll never forget the look on the doctor's face when I threw out all these different medical terms and told him he was full of it. I told him she wasn't going to die, and we were transferring her that day. This is the ultimate case of fake-it-until-you-make-it because, although I understood it on a high-level, I really didn't, but apparently I made enough of an impression on this doctor, who went pale white following my little speech. What I knew for sure was that he'd already given up on her, and I had to get her out of there. I called people I knew who could help me, made myself her power of attorney, and called my friend to drive me to Hershey Medical Center, where we had her transferred. It was a long journey, but she survived and is still very much alive and kicking today at seventy-two.

Things pretty much leveled out for a while once my mother recovered. My dad was focused on his malpractice lawsuit and my sister was enjoying quite a successful high school basketball career. She was amazing. She and her team took the State Championship her senior year, much to my parents' joy. They basked in her glory. I can still hear my dad yelling, "That's my kid." I was proud of her too, and it was such a relief to see some kind of happiness find its way back to our lives. Unfortunately, my sister's success was a comforting but temporary distraction from the truth of what was, and a new wave of mess began.

The next year over Christmas break, my dad tried to fight me and throw me against the wall, but I fought back for the first time, calling him everything in my heart I thought about him right to his face. I'll always remember it because he didn't know what to do at first, but of course, he wasn't having it and, being stronger than me, he threw me out the door onto the porch. I don't think I ever really went home after that. I bounced around, living with my boyfriend's family for a week or two and then moving in with my grammy. I found rides back and forth to school. I came home for my sister's graduation but was not welcomed at home. Ultimately, I ended up declaring full independence from my parents, got an apartment in Philadelphia off-campus, and applied for special hardship grants at school. These required being on the Dean's List and lots of paperwork, including testimony from family and friends, but I got all of it together and I did it. I was granted a half-tuition scholarship for the rest of my professional years. To this day, I am still paying off my loans, but what that borrowed money bought me was priceless.

As you may have guessed, the story of my dad does not end well. The final fall-out happened the summer before my sister went to college. I remember getting the call from my boyfriend's brother, Stephen. I learned that my mom and sister were already at the house. Apparently, my dad went some degree of crazy, and pulled a gun on my mother and my sister, causing my sister to flee the house, but paralyzing my mother in fear to the point where my sister had to literally pull her outside and hobble her down the street. They somehow got to my boyfriend's mom's house, which was right down the block. We called the police; he was jailed for a period of time but eventually got out and pretty much disappeared from our lives after that. It was a small town, so we always heard through the grapevine about what he was doing or who he was living with. He bounced around doing odd jobs and, at the end of his life, was a cook in the local diner. This still makes me laugh, as Sunday breakfasts were one of his favorite things, and he talked often when I was young about how much he enjoyed cooking for other people and would someday want to open his own breakfast joint. I guess this was as close as he got, but it still makes me happy to know he did it.

My father is currently very dead. He had pretty significant cardiovascular disease and had his first heart attack at the age of forty-two. He was given a stent and ordered to quit smoking and start eating right, which of course never happened.

The last time I saw him was right after I got a call from a woman who told me she was his girlfriend and that he had a stroke. Apparently, he named me power of attorney in his will, so I had to go speak with the doctor and make the decisions regarding the plan for the rest of his life. God is funny because the stroke completely took away his ability to speak, so when I saw him, he was alert, but couldn't speak a word. After meeting with the doctor, we decided to decline intubation and went with hospice care. He was dead in three days. There was a lot of healing that happened during that time for me, as I not only forgave him, but loved and prayed for him at the bedside through his transition. Losing a parent is a big deal, and losing one you had a bad relationship with but became responsible for at the end of that life is a whole other thing.

As you can only imagine, my mother had a good deal of emotional scars that she still carries to this day. It's hard to still see it, but I've accepted that it isn't going to change. My sister and I also carried much of the trauma into our adulthood and marriages. What I've shared with you here are the highlights, and there is so much more that is probably the content of another book, but know this – my sister and I have had to work very hard over the past two decades to heal these wounds, recognizing how much of what we absorbed as normal wasn't, but how it somehow became part of who we were deep inside of us. Those demons would emerge often, including when we would least expect. We quickly recognized how important it was for us to break the cycle of emotional abuse, including with each other. Having children opened my eyes to this in a way I am eternally grateful for, which really began my journey to understanding what self-love really means.

Self-love is tricky business, but it is everything. *Everything.* But here is the thing. It's probably not what you think it is. I believe when most people think about self-love, they think about treating themselves to a manicure or a girls' weekend, or something they think they need. Or maybe they think it's working out regularly and looking great as they age. I think those things can be manifestations of authentic self-love, but that's not the root of it. Self-love is knowing deep and true self-worth and that you are truly, truly loved unconditionally.

As I reflect on my life, it would have been so easy for me to play victim to my circumstances, trauma, and abuse. But that was never an option because I knew better. Being connected to that experience with Love when I was ten was everything for me and remains so up to this day – in fact, even more so. It was because I believed I was loved by my God that I never gave up. I never gave in. I believed I was going to get through it, that I was worthy of the good that was at the end of the mess. I returned to my faith again and again, I called on it on every single circumstance, and I trusted exactly what I heard: that everything was going to be OK. Not only did I believe it, but it was reinforced throughout the difficulty. It was shown to me in beautiful, simple ways through other people who I recognized were sent to me to support me, love me, show me the next step, or give me the next thing that kept me moving forward. Money I needed for school or rent or books seemed to come out of no-where when I needed it, from people, family, or a job opportunity on campus, and it was always just enough to get me through. I was always taken care of.

Let me be clear here: that didn't mean I wasn't suffering. It didn't mean I wasn't hurting. It doesn't mean I didn't have weeks of "how the heck am I going to do this?" It just meant I knew I would get through it, and most importantly, somewhere deep in my heart, I knew it was all part of some bigger plan, and these experiences were teaching me things. Some of them toughened me up while others softened my heart and allowed me to see someone or a situation differently than my peers. I always sought to learn something through it, even when I didn't like it or didn't agree with it or didn't want it.

This relationship I had with God was my anchor. It was everything to me, and at one point in high school and then again in college, I very seriously discerned entering the convent, to the point that I had to tell Mike what was going on in my head and heart. After a lot of soul searching and praying and one particular experience, I knew I was called to be a mother, but I never forgot what I heard that afternoon with my walk with Love. I had work to do here, and it would be revealed to me at the right time. So I just let go and chose to live my life, knowing it would show up exactly when it should.

A NEW CHAPTER

I carried all of this with me forward in my heart to my life and career. Once I completed my Pharm. D., I knew pretty quickly that retail pharmacy was not my cup of tea, so I pursued a residency training program in infectious diseases and moved from Philadelphia to Oklahoma. My boyfriend moved with me, and it began an entirely new chapter in my life. I wasn't making a ton of money as a resident, but it was one step closer to that job I wanted in the hospital as an infectious diseases clinical pharmacy specialist. Once I completed my residency, I landed my first job in Ann Arbor, MI, and for the first time in my life, I felt free, like I'd finally arrived. I had a good job that I loved, great people I worked with, met a wonderful group of friends. Mike and I were already engaged to be married, and we were planning our wedding at home. After the wedding, life seemed to move quickly for us after that. We moved back to Philadelphia, both found good jobs, and I found out I was pregnant in 2004. It was around this time that I began speaking on behalf of various pharmaceutical companies. I became intrigued about what seemed like a very glamorous life in the pharmaceutical industry. After my daughter Anna was born, I knew it was time for me to get out of hospital work. I was lucky enough to apply and interview for two jobs at two different companies, both that I had offered to me, both with exceptional people to work with, but I followed my heart and chose to work with a man named David. I saw so much light in him and I somehow knew it would be best for me to go to work with him without knowing why. I wasn't wrong.

David was indeed the gem I saw in him from the first time we met. He mentored me, guided me through this new terrain, helped me through all the endless transitions and changes that are the norm in the industry, empowered me as a working mother, positioned me for greatness, and gave me the confidence and the know-how to get to where I was going. He told me I had what it takes and I would be successful if I dug in. Which I did. You read the first chapter, right?

I eventually moved on from that company to take a crack at a position within a smaller sized, more nimble company, and then to a very small start-up in New York, eventually making my way to the company I work for now. It's been a wild ride. Through the last fourteen years, I've learned a lot about myself, about life, and about business. It has enabled me to have tremendous experiences and gave me many fantastic opportunities to explore the world, and I am grateful for every minute of all of it. But like all things, there is a shadow side, right? And I think we both know what that shadow looks like in the corporate world. The long hours, the travel, the politics, constant change, expectations, especially if you want to climb… and well, the truth is that it is what it is. It's part of the deal. You sign on and willingly, although perhaps unknowingly at first, extend your wrists for the golden handcuffs to be secured. At first, I didn't mind, because I was basking in it and enjoying all the fun gifts that came along with the binding: a corporate credit card, an executive assistant to book my trips in business class, lucrative salary, ability to experience wonderful places around the world, meet incredible people. I mean it when I say I have always felt so grateful for all of it, even on bad, busy, yucky days, I enjoyed the work and I worked my behind off to get it all.

What happened for me is that, over time, those handcuffs around my wrist began to feel just a little too tight. I was getting tired of the travel. Tired of the long hours and working weekends. I was tired of the late nights and the back-to-back meetings. I was tired of the politics and the drama. Not to mention, remember that little voice on the airplane when I was headed to Heathrow? It never really left. It would hear it in meetings. I would hear it while I was having fun at the bar after the meeting. I would hear it on vacation. It was always saying the same thing: you've got work to do and it's bigger than this. What I realized was, throughout this time, I didn't really hear the pull to leave my work or job per se, but what I did begin to see, over time, was that it was masterfully preparing me. It made me uncomfortable enough to be aware of what I was feeling, and from those moments, there were always new learnings. It enabled me to see something within someone I was working with that I needed to see for myself, or what I should and shouldn't take away from what I observed from their leadership. Over all those years, I began to see that layer after layer was being peeled back inside of me, not only showing me what I was capable of, but I also began to see my heart. The more I got to see and know what was in my heart, the more unsettled I became.

I began to ask questions like I shared in the previous chapter. "What am I really doing here? What am I working so hard and missing so much of my life for? Why am I not authentically happy? I have so much to be grateful for, but somehow it doesn't feel right. Why? What is the voice saying? What am I supposed to be doing if it's not this work? What do I do with this?

Little by little, I began to allow my heart to show me things I could be doing with my life and the real dreams I had within me.

THE MEETING

We were vacationing at the beach, and it was during a time when I was really feeling this unsettled place in my heart. I couldn't ignore it; it was full throttle. I was angry, frustrated, and I kept praying to be shown what was really going on. I asked to understand how I could possibly entertain these seemingly far away big dreams that were tantalizing and tormenting me. I asked for direction because I couldn't take it anymore. I was tired of feeling tired. I was tired of feeling confused and frustrated. I was tired of going back and forth with this voice and spending the energy to push it down and ignore it. I had enough.

On the second morning of our vacation, everyone was still asleep and I was awake, which was unusual for me considering I usually couldn't wait to sleep in. At the same time, I was emotionally spent, and I wasn't sleeping well anyway. I got up with a knot in my stomach, put my workout gear on, stepped outside onto the balcony, and took in the long stretch of beach in front of me. It was so beautiful and inviting. The sun was shining off the water, birds were squawking and diving into the ocean retrieving their breakfast, early morning runners were already glistening with sweat from their first few miles, and the air was thick and salty and sweet. I decided to take a long walk instead of going to the gym. I needed to breathe. I needed to think. I needed to take in the energy of the water and the ocean and figure out this knot in my gut. As I was walking and thinking and praying, the same thoughts circling round and round and round in my head, I started to get angry and sad. I felt hopeless. I could feel the anger rise in my chest and the tears of frustration welling up in my eyes, but it was at that moment that I decided to do something crazy. For the first time in too long of a time, I let go. I took a deep breath, opened my heart completely, and wept like a lost child.

I cried the kind of cry that you feel come from somewhere deep inside, the kind that hurts horribly but feels so good all at the same time. The ugly cry. The healing cry. I cried the kind of cry that had the power to wash off the layers of Band-aids piled up, giving air to the festering, infected, neglected wounds of my heart. I found I was more present than I had been in a long time. It was like everything around me was supercharged. I felt the heat of the sun on my skin. I heard the song in the breeze rushing through my hair and into my ears. I felt the pounding rhythm of ocean waves, the bass drum in sync with the melody of the breeze. I connected with each pebble of sand beneath my feet and the story within them. I felt the power and majesty of the God I know.

And then, with the eyes of my heart, I saw her. I saw my soul. I saw how I was hiding her, how I was choosing to deny her greatness and gifts. I was lying to her and suffocating her. I felt her. I saw how much pain she was in.

I saw that I was responsible for creating and enabling her suffering.

I saw everything I'd never dealt with that was deep inside of me. I saw how deep her wounds were. I saw how those unhealed wounds oozed the poison that infiltrated so many aspects of my life, breeding my confusion and frustration, enabling justification of the life I was living.

The poison was fear. Fear is the cancer that metastasized from my heart to head and ever so masterfully birthed lie after lie that I told myself about who I was. It was the poison that kept me safe. Secure.

And stuck.

Then I realized something else.

Even with all the bleeding wounds, my truth was simultaneously beautiful, and more than anything, it was incredibly powerful.

I consider that beach walk a timestamp of my life. I made a decision that morning. I would never neglect my soul again. I had to heal myself and to allow my soul to come forward to lead my life. I decided I would do everything I could to find the courage to do it. I became aware of the distinct "other" voice that was part of me too, the one that I was most familiar with, the one who learned early on that she needed to protect me and limit me so there wouldn't be another wound. I love her too – she got me to where I am today! But she's infected with fear, and I knew I had to be cognizant of when she was speaking to me. I also knew I would have to learn to silence her, because with the soul, there is no fight for the microphone. The soul doesn't fight for the limelight. She doesn't need to. She may be wounded, but she is very, very wise.

She has shown me that her wounds hold her power.

Most importantly, she speaks only the truth.

And I learned that the truth sets you free.

When you allow your soul to come forward, she will lead you to places you never knew you could go, and she will give you ideas that seem crazy, but when you learn to love and trust her enough to listen, you will come to understand that she knows the way. She knows because she is directly connected to something bigger than you, bigger than this realm we are incarnate in right now. You come to understand she is part of the Universe and comes directly from the One who breathed life into you and who gave you your unique gifts and purpose.

That week at the beach, she gently reminded me how powerful words are and that I was good at channeling her through them. This was the first taste for me of what life is like when your heart leads.

When we got home, I started my blog. My first post was about my beach walk, my talk with God, meeting my soul, and about the decision to follow my heart. I admitted I had no idea what I was doing, or what it would amount to, but I did it anyway. With each and every post I wrote, I let the words flow through me. I felt my heart sing, and I began to know and love and trust my voice. I found the courage to create a Facebook page for shorter posts that I wrote when I was told to do so, which grew pretty quickly (according to my standards). It felt good to write what was on my heart. I had many people reach out to me privately from this, sharing stories of how I inspired them by putting myself out there and that they now planned to do the same, or that my words shook something up deep inside of them. Then it began to feel purposeful, which lit up my heart. I began to pop up out of bed in the morning before work just to craft my posts for the day or the week. It was all flowing through me now. I was guided to a business coach and started a holistic wellness business I named Soul2SoulTransformations LLC. Little by little, I was healing, and my heart was leading the way. I felt overwhelmed with gratitude, and I began to find the confidence and courage to begin the journey to live life differently. I finally felt like I was on to something.

DARKNESS

Although I had a relationship with the Holy Spirit from a young age, I was very much grounded in the Catholic faith. I went to Catholic School for eight years and for most of my life, my family going to church was non-negotiable. However, shortly after I launched my blog and my coaching business, I became aware that of the fact that while in church, I wasn't inspired. I was annoyed. I was bored. Although I loved the connection I had to receiving communion and singing hymns, I otherwise felt, for lack of a better word, disengaged.

I also realized this has been going on for a while. My kids were also completely disengaged. I would look around the church and recognize that many other people were disengaged too and only going through the motions. I felt like we were a herd of cattle, following along mindlessly, speaking the words coded into our brains like programmed robots. I realized that many priests did the same, they read the words, but they had no feeling. No meaning. There was no heart behind what they were doing. Over time, this man behind the altar began to sound like Charlie Brown's schoolteacher and so I began to read the gospel on my own and meditated on what I read. When I listened to the homily, I realized two things:

1. I tuned in for the first two minutes and then found myself thinking about a million other things because what he was saying didn't mean anything to me.

2. I didn't agree with what was being said, and sometimes, what was being said infuriated me.

There were many other things that came into my awareness that weren't sitting right with me, and I was feeling more and more uncomfortable at mass. It bothered me.

And then, one day, Catholics everywhere woke up to the release of the Catholic church child molestation investigation report, and I pretty much drew a line in the sand. I read the full investigation and it was more than I could handle. I remained hopeful and waited anxiously for a heartfelt, emotionally charged, shame-filled, vulnerable speech or something that felt genuine from the bishop or priests, or someone. But in our dioceses, I only heard pathetic attempts at "apologies" from the pulpit and read coverup-like language in the paper and the church bulletin from the bishop to the families who were affected by the scandal. I never saw or heard what I believed was legitimate sorrow for what had happened. Just a whole lot of "so sorry for the disruption, nothing to see here…God loves you and forgives and you should too…move along now." The bottom line is, I lost the desire to be associated with anything that would dare try to smooth something so serious and painful over. I was disgusted, but more than anything, I felt duped. In Catholic school, I was taught priests were the chosen ones. They carried honor, and we should pray for them and never *ever* speak poorly of them because they are of God and called in a special way to do God's work (it's a sin, you know?).

This was not the work of the God I knew, and I could not stand by and pretend that it was for the sake of belonging.

I walked away.

So I think it's important to frame something for you here regarding where I am at this point in time: I'm in the middle of this awakening to myself, the religious institution I was part of since birth was no longer something I could identify with, and of course, all along, it's not like the ways of the material world got any better. It seemed like one day, I woke up with this new awareness of the weight of suffering being experienced in the world. Each day, there was something new: a child trafficking ring uncovered, learning that suicide and depression rates were soaring in adolescents, hearing about a young child diagnosed with bone cancer, a twenty-year-old dying of heroin overdose at a local high school, hate crimes, immigrant mothers seeking asylum, having to give up their screaming children to be put in cages because they feared for their lives. It felt never-ending. I was appalled, saddened, and terrified.

It's not that I was completely naïve to what was going on in the world before this time, it's just that since it didn't directly impact me, I didn't think too much about it because I didn't think there was anything I could do to change it. I chose to focus on myself and my life, my job, and my family, and leave the rest to God. But now, in a way I cannot say I experienced before, I saw and felt a new kind of pain and suffering. Pain and suffering that was taking place outside of me and all around me.

I actually heard myself asking:

Where am I? What is this place?

What am I doing here?

What am I working this hard for? Money? For me? For another vacation when all of this is going on around me? What am I teaching my kids? What are they going to inherit? Why is there so much suffering? What will my life amount to? What am I really here to do?

There has to be more to this story of this reality we are in.

I was carrying around all this new weight like a 100,000-pound sack on my heart and in my head for what felt like a very long time, and ultimately, it became unbearable to me. I was so angry and sad, my soul was dark, and I was literally dragging myself through my life. With each passing day and each new horrific event that was taking place, with each new sadness that would come to me, I could feel it all growing darker, and I was pulling farther and farther away from myself and the God I thought I knew and loved.

To top it all off, I was insanely miserable at work, and it just seemed to keep getting worse. Organizational changes were imminent. There was a real air of uncertainty and a whole lot of drama. I couldn't understand where God was. I couldn't understand why He would do this to me. Where was He? Why did He leave me? Why was I allowed to see this, to feel it all so deeply? Why is the loneliness so heavy, so unbearable? Is this what I get for connecting with myself? Agony? Did I do something wrong? Am I on the wrong path?

I found myself wanting to go home. Like home, home. Home to the voice in the alley. I realized sudden death didn't seem so bad, and in a weird way, it allowed me to feel better by not feeling at all. I was numb, going through the motions, doing what I needed to do. But inside I felt dead.

I was driving home from work one grey and rainy day, and I had this thought come into my mind: "So this is how it feels to question God's existence." For the first time in my life, I knew my faith was shaken, and I questioned what I believed.

A day or two later, I remember learning that the sister of a friend I used to work with got very sick and died rather suddenly, leaving behind a beautiful family of two young girls and a loving husband. I was up in my bedroom, unpacking my suitcase, and I hit a breaking point. I felt so deeply the pain and longing of those girls for their mother, the pain of feeling the loss and the desolation of her husband, and I realized I was very angry at God. I remember hearing someone say once, "It's OK to yell at God. He can take it." So I decided to do just that. I let him have it. I yelled out, my body shaking, hot tears rolling down my face,

Why? Why? Why???

Why so much pain? Why so much suffering?

Is this whole experience of this life some kind of sick joke?

Where are you? Why have you left me? This is not love, this is insanity. This is hell.

Please, please help me understand. Why?

Why…

I fell to my knees, bawling, wondering what was happening to me. I have never felt so scared and alone in my life. I actually started to wonder if I was going crazy.

Know this – when you call out to God, boldly baring pain in your soul, He hears you, and trust me when I say He answers. He most certainly did for me. Big time.

In an instant, overwhelming peace filled the room, and I became still. I stopped crying. I recognized the still, and I heard it. I heard the same gentle voice, the one that I knew from our walk in the alley that day. I heard, *"Tammy, I love you. You know this. You know Me. It's time now. Everything is going to be OK."*

So began my journey. The journey to my answer. The journey to the truth. The journey to what I'm here to do with my life and how I will fulfill my purpose. It is the reason I exist, the reason I experienced everything I have up to this point. It is the reason I am writing this book, and very likely the reason you are reading it.

LIVING MY TRUTH

For me, my journey has been like drinking through a fire hose – it's been intense, but wonderful. Here is what I have learned so far:

That beautiful soul I met on my walk on the beach? She is healing. Every day, she is healing, one wound at a time. To heal her, I had to learn to love her and trust her in a way that relies heavily on unconditional love from God. She and I are one. This doesn't mean the "other" little voice of fear doesn't pop up. She's a bold one and a baddie. She's tough. We love her anyway, but are quick to tell her to go sit in the corner. We have work to do – the work and God's grace that comes through me from the healed wounds of my soul. As each heals and seals over, it becomes a transmuted beacon of light – powerful healing light that filters through my pores, my hands, through my eyes, and into every soul I am here to touch, inspire, love, and heal and which in turn helps me to heal further too.

I have learned that I have special gifts that the God I know gave me and expects me to use, including channeling the Holy Spirit into words. I can feel, hear, and see things others cannot, and my job is to speak what I feel, see, and hear regardless of how weird it may sound or how difficult it might be to say. I have always had these gifts, but now, I do not deny them. I love them, I acknowledge them, and they serve me and the others I touch. I trust myself and I trust the voice, and the more I trust the voice and let it speak to me, the clearer it becomes. It has been a long journey to write and declare this, but one that has been worth every minute. And I know, it is indeed my time.

I have been told that now and in the coming years, many souls have to become awakened, and I am here to help trigger their awakening. Upon doing so, I am here to guide them home – home to themselves, home to unconditional Love, and home to their truth, just like I found mine. Because it is in our truth that we find our purpose, and living out our purpose is what is going to change and heal the world and our planet. One person, one beautiful soul at a time.

This all came together for me in an instant, as I realized that God gifted me with the understanding of why I needed to go through that painful experience of feeling God's absence; why did I have to feel the darkness and experience the depth of what I saw and felt? Because without it, I couldn't understand and see others the way I do now. Now I know firsthand how people who don't know or don't believe in Love at all may be feeling or seeing and why they might question their existence.

I also understand that even if they once did have a strong and stable faith, how easy it can be for this world to lead them to question God's existence, and how difficult that is, how terrifying and lonely that can be, even though often, just like everything else, it is part of the bigger plan. I understand completely why they hurt, how they are tired, angry, sad, frustrated, and lonely. I understand the depth of that loneliness. I understand how they may be asking where they are and why they are probably thinking that this life must be some kind of sick joke. I also understand how easy it is to get caught up in garbage, in false gods that surround us, and why they can be so very tempting.

They are so readily available and easy; they exist to distract us from the truth, to give us pleasure, promising freedom from the loneliness and the pain, because distractions just for a while are such a gift when you feel that kind of darkness. The problem is that we will always wake up empty the next day. We know this. We recognize it. But what else is there to do? So we do it over and over and over again. We wake up and search for happiness, joy, and contentment in the world, but when we keep coming up empty, it makes sense that we begin to search for relief.

If you are paying attention, you will notice that it is happening all around us every day, more than ever before. We are lost.

We are disconnected.

The things you think you are seeking are not what you need, and that's why it feels so hard to put your finger on them. The answer is not out in the world. It's inside of you, and that invisible force making you uncomfortable, shaking up you and your life in the midst of your big plans, is real. All it means is you are loved and you are chosen. We are all chosen. If you are brave enough to decide to take this journey, I can tell you first-hand that it will change your life forever. You too will become awakened and connected to the truth, of not only who you are, how powerful you are, and what you are here to do, but to the incredible, magical world that exists, a world that will leave you filled with wonder and awe, and that holds limitless abundance that is yours for the taking.

It is not on some magical island or remote resort.

It is all here, inside of you and present in the extraordinary of everyday life.

CHAPTER 3

THE ROADMAP TO UNLOCK THE GOLDEN HANDCUFFS

"You were born a child of light's wonderful secret, you return to the beauty you have always been."
— Aberjhani, Visions of a Skylark Dressed in Black

When my children were younger, reading to them before bed was my favorite thing in the world. We would pick a book together, snuggle into bed, and dive in. As young babies, it would be a few quick books like *The Berenstain Bears Get the Gimmies* (my daughter's favorite) or *Otis* (my son's favorite). As they got older, we would begin with one of them reading to me for practice, but they would tire quickly and ask me to read to them. I would lie there reading until I heard their breath become softer, falling into a sweet rhythm of peaceful sleep – my cue to exit. I would stealthily untangle arms and legs from mine and slip out of bed, carefully avoiding clothes, Legos, and game pieces, drearily dragging myself into my own bed to rest. Having a fifteen and twelve-year-old now, I realize those were precious times indeed.

There was a book that I bought for me and my son to read called *The Key to Extraordinary* by Natalie Lloyd that will forever be one of our favorites. It's a sweet, fun story filled with twists, turns, and lots of magic. The story revolves around the main character Emma, who is twelve years old, and her Grandmother Blue, short for Bluebell Althea, who is raising Emma and her brother Topher, as their mother died two years before. Emma and her family come from a lineage of ancestors who did amazing things with their lives – each learned their destiny through a dream that they call the Destiny Dream, which provided a message and clues to their extraordinary destiny. Her ancestors included brilliant scientists, war spies that saved the lives of thousands of people, and even famous country music singers. Each person was required to document their dream and how they lived their extraordinary life in a book called the *Book of Days*, which was passed on from generation to generation.

Emma is desperately waiting for her Destiny Dream. When it finally arrives, she finds she is very intrigued but also very, very underwhelmed. She dreams of a key and a bundle of flowers – specifically a daisy, a violet, and a single red rose. Her dream kicks off the journey of a lifetime, complete with her realization of incredible magic that surrounds her and is within her, which she finds with the help her family and friends, including new ones she meets along the way. In the end, she understands not only the meaning of her dream, but also the meaning of her life, who she truly is, and the power that resides in knowing this and what she is to do with that knowing. I loved this book. I cried like a baby at least twice, but especially at the end. I felt so connected to this simple but beautiful story. Here's why.

I wrote this book to awaken your heart to understand that you too are called to an extraordinary destiny. Although we don't necessarily have a Destiny Dream to give us clues and a roadmap to that destiny, through my journey, I recognized there is a way to know what we are here to do and it begins with unearthing and falling deeply in love with who we truly are, revealing the beauty of who we have always been. There is a process to this unearthing, and this book will walk you through it so can understand what is happening and where you may be in the process. You'll also learn what you can expect moving forward, but most importantly, that everything you experienced up to this point was chock-full of purpose and learnings that you needed to experience to do what you are being called to do.

Remember how I mentioned that the feeling of being unsettled is the beginning? This is what I call *the invitation*, and we will explore it in depth in Chapter 4. Recognition of this part of the journey is critical because it can be very tricky to notice depending on how connected you are to both yourself and to that something bigger than you. Understanding the invitation requires a different kind of awareness and understanding of dharma or vocation. Once the invitation is understood and acknowledged, it requires an RSVP with a pure, true heart and open mind, which serves as the confirmation you are ready for *transformation*, not just change, and fully understand the difference between the two.

In Chapter 5, we will discuss ego versus self, the importance of taming ego, and learning how to connect fully to self. In the story, Emma learned she had access to a magic Telling Vine. The Telling Vine was a vine with buttercup-like blooms that when placed up to her ear with a clear question, clear intention, and an open mind and heart, it allowed her connection to her ancestors and her mother, who provided her with guidance and support of her journey. Our magic Telling Vine is prayer and meditation, which is not nearly as hard as you may think.

We will explore prayer and meditation, likely in a different way than you have heard before. Regardless if you have been praying your whole life, or have never prayed or meditated before, I want to assure you that this chapter will break it down for you in a simple and straightforward way. I think you will be surprised at how easy it will come to you. Like anything new, it may take practice and it may be uncomfortable at first, but once you get started and do it consistently, you will see how effortless it is, how much magic lies within it, and how innate it really is to your being.

Things get really interesting from here on out. In Chapters 6, 7, and 8 we will explore transformation, awakening, and activation, which is unique to you and different for every soul, but simply put, it is the process of remembering who you really are and seeing the world and the people within it with new eyes. It ultimately results in living with a deeper level of connection to the world. I want to be very clear here that this is big and often difficult work. Transformation alone brings us to a place that can feel very scary, lonely, and exceptionally vulnerable. Getting through these three phases can take on many forms and carry a lot of energy, and thereby can be quite exciting, but also overwhelming. Therefore, recognizing it is happening and where you are in the process is critical, and knowing how to self-manage through it can be the lynchpin to not feeling crazy and not feeling so overwhelmed that it paralyzes your progress. You can definitely go about managing all of it on your own, but having a strong and wise spiritual guide with you through this time is generally a good thing and frankly, sometimes very necessary.

Once you emerge from transformation into the new world and you are getting comfortable in your new skin following your awakening, it's time to really start connecting to and activating the innate spiritual gifts or powers every soul has been gifted with upon its creation. You see, an awakened heart is a powerful one that is super stoked and chomping at the bit to set forth to discovering purpose, dharma, or vocation. It's a time of "spiritual training" of sorts. Moving forward, you will be required to call on these gifts and to develop them in a way that enables them to re-establish themselves as a natural part of who you are. They have always been there – it's just now you are aware of them in a different way. Learning how to use them correctly and harnessing their power is fun and exciting. Lots of awe and wonder here!

The final step in this process is called *unmasking*. Once transformed and activated, you will recognize that you have developed the spiritual aptitude, courage, and confidence to evaluate your life in a new way. I call it unmasking because what we are really doing is unmasking your ego by naming your fears and bravely stepping through them as the illusion that they are into the arms of your true self. In Chapter 8, we will discuss how, in coming face to face with ego, we begin to understand how it has generated fear and how fear has blinded us to our gifts and purpose. This allows us to see clearly, usually for the first time, how our lives up to this point have been preparing us for this next step and how our story contains all the clues we need to know exactly what we need and want to do next that will fill our lives with authentic joy and happiness.

In Chapter 9, we will discuss *surrender and emptying*. This is where it is of utmost importance to understand that the gifts of authentic happiness, joy, peace, fulfillment, and abundance found in purposeful living are not only a result of what we do but *how we do it*. In this chapter, we will explore the lives of two souls who mastered surrender and emptying – Mother Teresa and Mahatma Gandhi – and through examining their lives, we come to understand how powerful surrender is and how it results in almost effortless manifestation of abundance and impact that truly changes the world.

Finally, in Chapter 10, we will revisit ego and true self in the context of flow and resistance following transformation, because despite all of our work in this sacred process, ego never dies.

With all this growth comes natural challenges, and I would be doing you a disservice if we did not spend at least a little time discussing some of the difficulties you may face as you learn to become more of your true self and strive to live your truth. Chapter 11 includes some tips and tricks to help you through, but is also a place where a spiritual life coach can really change the game and ensure the clarity you had with unmasking is trusted fully and pulled through.

Obviously, you may be picking this book up and know that you are just beginning this journey, or you may recognize that you are somewhere along the way. You may want to jump right to that chapter to explore it and see what's coming. Feel free to do this, but I want to encourage you to consider going back to the previous chapters at some point, taking your time to explore each step. You can see what resonates with you, what else comes up for you that you may not have thought of, and what you may need to explore further along the way.

Lastly, as you are beginning your journey to designing your own *Book of Days*, you will need, well, a book. You should keep a journal. It is a requirement for this journey. Journaling is so critical because many times, our energy is channeled through our hearts in words our voice cannot or fears to say out loud. The journal is your sacred space to express and document what you may not be ready to say. It also serves as a great tool for reflection, which you will soon learn is a requirement for spiritual growth.

There is so much to explore, so much to learn, and so much to dive into.

Let's begin.

CHAPTER 4

RECOGNIZING THE INVITATION

"It is not more vacation we need, it is more vocation."
— Eleanor Roosevelt

Following my experience in the alley and being raised Catholic, Jesus became very special to me early in my life. Knowing Him the way I did allowed me to see Him differently when I learned the stories of His life in church or in Catholic school. One of my favorite stories is the Wedding at Cana. Essentially, it is when Jesus is told by His mother Mary that it is time to begin to fulfill His vocation. This story is so important that it earned a spot in the Luminous Mysteries of the Rosary in 2002, when Pope John Paul II added it to the already existing fifteen mysteries.

If you have no idea what I'm talking about, of course you can easily read all about it in the Bible, but here is how I hear it and what is relevant for our purposes right now: at this time, basically Jesus was a young, happy, thirty-ish year-old man who was just beginning His public ministry. He, His mother, and few of His closest friends were attending a wedding, probably a relative. Everyone was dancing and having a blast at the wedding when they realized that the wine had run out. So if you like weddings like I do, you understand the magnitude of this problem. I mean, who doesn't love a good wedding with good wine and good music being surrounded by family celebrating love? To me, it is truly one of the best joys and best experiences of this human life.

Jesus totally felt the same, I know it. The thing that I have always seen first with Jesus was that He was human.

Think about it – what would you be doing at thirty years old at your cousin's wedding? I know Jesus was out there dancing. He was drinking and having fun. Until the wine ran out. Mary, not wanting her family to be embarrassed by this awful turn of events and knowing all about her son, asks Jesus to intercede. From John 2:3-5, NIV:

Mary: "They have no wine."

Jesus: "Oh Woman, what has this to do with me? My hour has not come."

What I see and hear:

Mary: Jesus, come over here. There is a problem.

Jesus (sweaty from dancing, runs over to his mother): What's up?

Mary: We have to do something. They ran out of wine and are going to be super embarrassed. I know you can help.

Jesus: Come on, Mom. Can't you see I'm out here having fun? This really isn't my problem. Do I have to?

To which Mary probably gives him the mom look, walks away, brings over the servants, and says to them, "Do whatever he tells you." (John 2:3-5, NIV)

Moms. They have that power, don't they? All it takes a look and you know what you better do.

Jesus, obeying his mother, tells the servants to bring him large jugs filled with water. He prays over the jugs and then orders the servants to draw some out and take it to the chief waiter. The waiter, having no idea where it came from tastes it and calls over the bride and groom saying, "Um, yeah, so why the heck are you serving the good wine now? Where was this a few hours ago? Why didn't you serve this first? Don't you know the rule – you serve the good stuff first and the cheap stuff later after everyone is drunk?"

In Christian tradition, this is considered Jesus's first public miracle. There are lots of deep and beautiful interpretations of this miracle, things like, "*It's always darkest before the dawn, but good things are on their way,*" and that Jesus is, "*the good wine.*" I like all of those, but I have to tell you that all I see is Jesus listening to his mom, and naturally doing what He does and what He will always do when we seek Him out. He takes a problem and replaces it with a solution that exceeds our expectations, because well, He's Love and that's what Love does.

Jesus' life is a perfect example of a human being living out His *vocation*. If you were Buddhist, you might say Jesus knew and fulfilled His *dharma* perfectly. These two terms can become very complicated very quickly. If you were to look up *dharma*, you would learn that, for Hindus, it is "the moral order of the universe and a code of living that embodies the fundamental principles of law, religion, and duty that governs all reality."

Vocation in Christianity is considered to be the sacred duty we are here to fulfill in our lifetime and that we are expected to do by living righteously with the highest moral conduct aligned to God's plan for our lives and for the world. Being human beings and the highest living form of life on earth, we can live out many vocations (or dharmas) that will take place over our time here on earth. Each, if done and lived well, brings us closer to enlightenment or heaven, so that we can return home and again become one with the Love and truth that we really are.

Dharma or vocation is simply our purpose. It is the reason your heart is beating and the reason you have breath in your lungs right now. It's what you are here to do, and whatever that thing is, it is absolutely critical to the future of the world.

WE ARE SPIRITUAL BEINGS HAVING A HUMAN EXPERIENCE

One thing I am not going to do in this book is go in-depth into different spiritual philosophies or religions, as there are many and frankly, they will distract us from our purpose here. In fact, one objective of this book is to make the concept of spirituality and connection to something bigger than ourselves as simple and as non-judgmental as possible. So everyone, regardless of where you are on your journey, can come to understand the key role spirituality has in our lives and give themselves permission to explore it, if for nothing more than for the mere fact that you are alive. Spirituality is part of who we are. It is our birthright and inherent to our beings. One of my favorite sayings is, "we are spiritual beings having a human experience." Even if you do not believe in God, I will still say that you are likely more spiritual than you think, you just don't realize it. Maybe not yet, anyway.

Realizing and acknowledging you *are* a spiritual being is the beginning. We are invited every day to connect to something bigger than ourselves. I'm not talking about going to church. I'm talking about seeking to understand why we may be feeling really uncomfortable with life these days – that *is* the invitation. Being uncomfortable is Love's gentle way of telling us, "Hey, I have bigger plans for you. Want to see what they are?" All we have to do is be aware enough to pause and consider it and agree to see where it takes us.

In Chapter 2, we talked about my day on the beach, where I finally opened my heart to really see and explore the nagging inside of me and found the strength to answer the invitation. From that story, hopefully, I illustrated that it is often harder than it sounds to say yes, and even harder to be aware that this is what you are being asked to do. It's not like you're getting some magical spirit to appear to you, saying that you have this life mission that you need to fulfill. Even if that did happen, you would probably question your sanity anyway. The truth is that often we have to be pushed to where we break, to where we have no choice but to consider calling out to something bigger than us to help us along. Sometimes even then, we don't realize the invitation before us.

We all have a life mission to fulfill, but life keeps us busy and distracted, and our ego rules our world. We are going to talk a lot about ego in this book with good reason. Ego keeps us so grounded to this reality and attached to our own desires, needs, and wants that we lose our connection to who we really are. But it is when we recognize that perhaps we are busy for the sake of being busy that we begin to question what we are doing the work for. When we feel unfulfilled in our lives or our work is when we hear the whisper, "Wait, something isn't right. There has to be more than this."

This often also manifests as us "hitting a wall," despite our best attempts to reach our goals. Maybe it seems that, no matter how hard you are trying to see your way to that next promotion or find that next job, nothing seems to be lining up and more often than not, you are finding yourself in this constant state of frustration and confusion. That's how it was for me. Of course, I totally ignored it and pushed through it. Nothing was going to stop *me*.

Do you hear it? Me. It was all about me. It was all ego-driven work and desire. But then inevitably, I was pushed to a place where I would have no choice but to see the writing on the wall and believe that what I was hearing was real: "I have bigger plans for you."

Finally, our little conscious brains start to put it together. "Hmm. Maybe it is time for something new. Or I need something to feel good and excited about again. Or I didn't think about that before, but...what about this..."

Those thoughts stem from the subconscious, where our soul is gently nudging and informing us we are ready for our next dharma – our next step in fulfilling our vocation. All we have to do next is say yes and connect to it with an open heart. Then, the adventure begins.

CHAPTER 5

CONNECTION

"In the attitude of silence the soul finds the path in a clearer light, and what is elusive and deceptive resolves itself into crystal clearness. Our life is a long and arduous quest after Truth."
— Mahatma Gandhi

H ave you ever traveled to Disney World? If not, I highly suggest you add it to your bucket list, like, now.

Like anything, it is not for everyone. But if you want to bring a little magic into your life and want to remember what it felt like to be ten-years-old in about thirty seconds, I suggest you give it a go.

We have been Disney Vacation Club members for a number of years now, and it is literally one of our favorite places on earth. The more you go, the more memories become embedded in the experience, and the more it continues to become even more magical with every passing year.

The latest and greatest ride in the Animal Kingdom park is "Avatar: Flight of Passage," *not* to be confused with "Na'vi River Journey," which is a very slow-moving and beautiful boat ride that lasts about eight minutes. My son and I spent four hours waiting in line for this one after "Flight of Passage." Trust me, it is much less exciting and exhilarating. Some words of wisdom – *do not* get on this ride after "Flight of Passage" and *do not* get in line without a fast pass. You're welcome.

"Flight of Passage" is an absolutely next level experience in terms of rides that exist on earth. No exaggeration here. The re-creation of Pandora in the park will truly knock your socks off, but the ride is simply incredible. As usual, Disney nailed it. I would even go as far as to suggest that if you are going to Disney and won't be returning anytime soon after, you should make it a point to get on this ride, even if you spend half the day waiting in line. It's totally worth it.

The movie is also one of my favorite movies of all time. If you live under a rock and for some reason haven't seen it, make plans right now to go rent it this weekend. It's long, but you won't even notice or care. Honestly, I think it should be required watching for all of humankind.

The film is set in the mid-twenty-second century, where humans are colonizing the lush habitable moon of Pandora, since we depleted all of Earth's resources. It just so happens that Pandora was found to be very rich in a resource called unobatanium, which is a superconductor that is worth millions and millions of dollars back on earth. Driven by greed and ignorance, humans are doing what we humans tend to do best – destroying the planet along with it the indigenous Na'vi people who inhabit it. The Na'vi are a species of ten-foot-tall, blue-skinned, sapient humanoids that live in harmony with nature and worship their mother goddess named Eywa. Due to the poisonous atmosphere on Pandora, scientists create "Avatars," which are genetically engineered hybrid human-Na'vi bodies that are operated or controlled from the brain of a remotely located human in order to interact and learn from the Na'vi people and experience Pandora. Each avatar is genetically programmed to its respective human controller and essentially, when connected, the controller lives through the avatar and is otherwise completely unaware of his or her human body while linked.

OK, I'm going to try to sum up a three-hour movie in a paragraph, but I hope you get the point. Lots of drama happens to our main character Jake Sully, a paraplegic former Marine, who finds himself in his avatar in Pandora, alongside Dr. Grace Augustine, the head of the Avatar Program. One day, while collecting biological data with Grace and other fellow scientists, Jake's avatar is attacked by one the many scary creatures native to Pandora called a thanator, causing him to run away into the forest, where he meets and is rescued by Neytiri, a female Na'vi. Jake has got some serious magic going on as he embodies his avatar state, so witnessing it and understanding it is a sign, Neytiri brings him back to her tribe and to her mother, who also happens to be the Na'vi's spiritual leader.

She too recognizes the sign and orders her daughter to initiate Jake into their society. Neytiri trains and teaches him the way of the Na'vi people, including the critical rite of passage of taming a powerful banshee, a wild, fierce-flying creature who enjoys the freedom of doing whatever it wants and accessing some of the most incredible parts of Pandora. Taming a Banshee requires connecting to it spiritually and physically, head to tail, and is a fight to the death. If the Na'vi warrior wins, the banshee submits and they gain control over the banshee forever, ensuing a lifelong relationship of trust, love, and limitless exploration and protection. To make a very long story short, Jake gets initiated into the tribe, and he and Neytiri fall in love and choose each other as mates. He tames a big, bad, powerful, awesome banshee, and following a long and very dramatic battle, he ends up saving Pandora. All humans are expelled and sent back to Earth, and Jake is permanently transferred into his avatar with the aid of the magic of Eywa and the Tree of Souls.

Ok. So what does this have to do with you and this book?

Think of it this way – you are a spiritual being who exists in a human Avatar here to explore Earth. The journey you are on that began the day your soul was born into your human body here on earth is the same as Jake's consciousness being transported into his avatar in Pandora. Your body is your soul's vehicle to explore and learn while alive on this earth. Jake's avatar was programmed to do whatever Jake told it to do, much the same as our avatar is programmed to be controlled by our soul, which feeds our consciousness with love and truth to guide us to fulfill what we are here to do.

Jake could never understand Pandora or explore it the way he needed to without being birthed into his Avatar, and it is the same for us. This planet, our Pandora, is foreign to us too when we first arrive, but we are given gifts to help us navigate, explore, learn, and grow here on Earth. As Jake was filled with awe and wonder of Pandora, we too should be amazed by what this Earth has within it and on it, for it is a taste of the love of our creator. We too have a very specific purpose to fulfill, and we are expected to do just that while we are here. Jake never intended to stay on Pandora – but yet he found his purpose was to save the Na'vi people.

Here on Earth within our Avatar, we will meet our banshee, or our ego, and just like on Pandora, it is a rite of passage. Just like the Na'vi do on Pandora, we seek it out to protect us from the perceived threat of Earthly thanators and other predators, which we meet early in our lives. Once we connect to it, it too becomes a lifelong partner. It is a wild beast who sees you as a weak being and it believes it exists to protect you. It knows its way around your mind, it smells your wounds and very aptly comes up with a story of how you have been let down by your avatar and your creator, but not to worry, because *it won't let it happen to you again.* It serves an important purpose, but before we can use it to its greatest potential, we must tame it. The problem is that, just like the banshee on Pandora, our ego does not and will never wish to be tamed.

Our banshee sees Earth as the end-all, the only thing that is real. It is material, selfish, dramatic, and worries only about itself and its perceived power. It only wants one thing – more power. It lives in a state of fear and lack, and teaches us that fear and lack is the truth and that it is because of others that we suf-fer. If we never recognize it and learn to tame it, it will convince us that we have no power, that we are victims of this reality and will die just as we are, until we forget who we are and from which we came. The ego in its loud, boisterous, fear-driven cadence effectively drowns out the quiet, gentle whisper of the soul, who patiently waits for the right moment to speak to us.

When we can't hear our soul, our true guide, we become lost, confused, unsettled, and stuck. We forget what we are here to do. We forget we have this direct connection to the One who loves us and who created us. Being disconnected leads us to become so disillusioned, so caught up in ourselves that we can't hear or see anything other than what is right in front of us. We forget that our avatar and time on this Earth is just a temporary reality.

Taming our banshee is also a fight to the death, for if we suc-cumb to ego, we will expend our energy here and die to it. But if we tame it, we gain control of our lives and ultimately can re-direct the course of our lives to purpose. The Universe that surrounds us is in full support of this and is always working for you and recreating itself around you for your good, because your life here ultimately contributes to the good of the world.

It's like having the most incredible network of love and light to guide and support you. Just as Jake's connection to the Na'vi on Pandora was no less real than his connection to human beings when he was back on Earth, it is the same with us. Our connection to our soul, which directly comes from and is connected to the infinite wisdom of God, is just as real and readily accessible within us and within other souls here on earth. We have to rise together and tame our egos, because when we do, we remind others they can do it too, and in turn show each other that there is nothing to fear.

A tamed banshee united with the soul in our avatar is like connecting Ewya of Pandora with the eternal power of our God. Now we not only remember what we are here to do, but we know exactly how to do it in the realm our avatar lives in. The banshee serves us by knowing and reminding us of the reality we are in, and the soul reminds us of who we really are, from which we came and will return, the powers we have been gifted, and what we are here to do, fully supported with an infinite amount of energy and love from our Source. United together, tamed ego and soul are a force to be reckoned with, and ultimately serve our highest good and the good of the world. This is the secret sauce – to know and love and honor both and courageously go out into the world and wield their power fearlessly.

THE OTHER SIDE

Can you see now the power that lies in knowing that we are spiritual beings having a human experience, not the other way around? It's really that simple. If you do not tame the ego and stop it from silencing your soul's voice and the gifts that lie within your avatar, you will forever be living in an illusion of fear and lack created by ego.

So, how do you get there? How do you find your soul and connect to it? How do you tame your ego and tap into the power of that connection on the other side? Jake was transported into his avatar by connecting himself to a machine that moved him in between realities. Our modality to jump back and forth to the other side is *meditation*. In meditation, we learn how to create an environment where the ego loses its privilege to run rampant so we can link our consciousness and soul. This connection opens up a whole other world, as the soul comes forward to show us the truth.

The soul knows the way. It knows who we are, how loved we are, and how fear is illusion. It knows Love is unconditional and *exactly* what we need to bring along with us in order to fulfill our purpose. Just as Jake spent a good amount of time getting to know Pandora and the ways of the Na'vi people through training with Neytiri, we too have to undergo some training in the new world we have been opened to. Because we've been disconnected for so long, we have to spend time getting to know how to explore the earth using our soul and Source energy. We have to learn how to survive differently, to see and uncover the magic that exists on Earth, but most importantly how to keep the ego reigned in. By doing so, we can fully explore and enjoy our time here on Earth, because we are learning and remembering who we are, how to truly love and trust ourselves again as we go back to who we were when we were born. Think about the last time you saw a young child playing alone in their room. We are quick to say he or she has a "vivid imagination," but maybe it is only that they see life through the eyes of their innocent souls still firmly connected to unconditional Love and the endless magic that resides within it.

Meditation and prayer are innate. It's part of the programming of your human avatar – you just have to access it. You can be guided *how* to do it, but for the most part, you *already know how*. In fact, you probably do it more than you think you do. One book I love that nails this concept and beautifully untangles the delicate nature of religion from spirituality in order to create a simple, practical guide to connection, regardless of what you believe, is *The Power of the New Spirituality* by William Bloom. It is the best I've read to date regarding how to connect to what he calls "the wonder and energy of life." Bloom offers three "Golden Keys," or three key practices to give you awareness of your innate ability to connect to your spirit as well as deepen and fully integrate them into your life. The three keys are very simple and straightforward: *connection with the wonder and energy of life, the power of self-reflection,* and *being of service to others.* These three behaviors are at the heart of "new spirituality" and can be found in any and all spiritual traditions and religions that exist in the world today. Let's begin with connection.

CONNECTING TO THE WONDER AND ENERGY

We own a lake house tucked away on a little nature preserve in the Pocono Mountains. It is my favorite place on earth. Why?

Because it is where I easily and readily connect to the wonder and energy of life. Here is what I mean.

We usually head up to the house on a Friday night or early Saturday morning. When we do, I am usually subconsciously carrying something with me from the week of work. As soon as my car turns the corner and I see the lake, my soul sighs. It steps forward, hugs me, and I smile. I get settled in, usually go for a long walk with my dog through the community and into the woods, and I always end up on the same bench by the water where I fully and completely connect to Love, who I call Jesus. It's like my direct channel just opens.

I talk like I'm talking to my best friend in the world, because I am. There are no actual words that leave my lips, only thoughts of my day, my week, what is bothering me, what I can't figure out, what I'm sad about, mad about, or whatever. I will tell you this much – I have never left there not knowing the answer or feeling like everything was OK, because it always is, and it always will be. I am just reminded and gently loved back to remembering this is the case. I have written some of my most favorite prayers here because my ego doesn't even exist there. This is the simplicity of connection.

You don't need a lake house to do this – it literally can be done anywhere at any time, and you can do it too. In fact, I'm going to bet you do it more than you think you do. Take a minute and think of a time when you were maybe having a conversation with a friend or walking outside and you caught a beautiful sunset, the kind that makes you pause, forget what you were saying, or even stop talking. You just observe, breathe, and take it in. Some other common examples are the feelings you get at the beach or around any body of water, seeing your dog bound toward you when you get home from work, or watching your kids sleep. You feel something shift, soften, and your heart sings. It is like reconnecting to something you *know*, something special and beautiful. It feels happy, peaceful, wonderful, and you wish it could stay around forever. This is a very normal experience, and it is a very *spiritual experience*. That change of perspective and gift of the release of what your mind has been wrestling with is God's way of getting your attention and creating the space for your soul to speak, "Hi, love. It's OK. Everything is going to be OK. Just stop. Pause. Breathe here with me for a minute. Let me refresh you." When we learn to recognize these moments and become aware of how we feel when they are happening, we can appreciate them differently, sink into them, and feel grateful for them. In turn, they become intensified, allowing us to fully take in the energy and grace available in that moment that will light up our hearts and reconnect us to unconditional Love that surrounds us and lives within us. It's all Love, and my friends, that's all God is. Love. Always available, always inviting you to connect.

SELF-REFLECTION AND SERVICE

Self-reflection, especially when coupled with service, is a very powerful spiritual tool. Think about how good it feels when you think about something you know you did that was good, that came from your heart. Now think about how great it feels when you did that something good for someone else, and you saw them light up when you did it for them. Pretty amazing feeling, right? It lifts you up, charges you in a different way, and makes you feel alive and happy. And when you reflect on it, your heart and soul remembers and identifies with that feeling, making you want more of it. We begin to recognize and understand how and why things done for ourselves could never carry the same feeling, the same authentic happiness and joy. This is because, in loving service to another person, you subconsciously connect soul to soul, reminding each other that you are both part of and connected to something much bigger than just you and this temporary reality. Through the power of service fueled by Love, we connect to and ultimately heal each other.

When I began to write and I stopped being afraid of the voice and what would happen to me (ego) if I wrote what it was telling me when it was coming through, I felt incredibly alive and full of energy. It was crystal clear, like I could take on the world with love and compassion. I would be up writing my blog at insane hours and would wake with a start and a spring in my step the next morning, coffee not included. One morning, I reflected on how it felt the night before when I was writing and how it felt as I was getting ready to go into my "other" life at work. There was quite a difference. I realized my office work felt cold, heavy, and sterile. It felt controlled and like I had to mask into my "professional-self." It felt fake and frankly, at this point, silly. I could easily put on the mask, but why? For what? I was alive and I wanted to stay feeling that way. I realized I was at the crossroads of the work I was doing and the work I really knew I needed to pursue. I didn't want to put on my mask. I didn't want to switch gears and go into the office. I couldn't speak the things I wanted to speak there as professional Tammy until I decided that I would.

SOUL FUEL

I knew that practicing and implementing these three simple golden keys of spirituality changed my life, so maybe they could change others' lives too. One day as I was driving into work, I thought about what would happen if I brought these concepts to where we just might need it most – at work. You know, the place we spend ninety percent of our lives? The place that many of us worked our tails off at every day? There.

Ironically, I learned that there was an opportunity at an upcoming national meeting, where the company wanted to offer morning workshops that focused on hot topics like work-life balance. I learned that there was one on mindfulness. *A-ha*! I decided to put my money where my mouth was and listen to my heart. Even though I was slammed, I agreed to conduct the workshop. I was paired with a woman who had a Ph.D. in mindfulness, and we came up with a one-hour program to kick off the meeting. I was so excited planning and thinking about it!

The morning of the workshop, I was awake early and so insanely energized. I literally couldn't wait. When it was my turn to speak and lead the exercise we agreed upon, it was like something took over. I let go and enjoyed every single moment in front of that room. I was channeling something new. I was beaming from the inside out, and I could feel every person in that room beaming light right back to me. The feedback I received made me have to go back to my room to catch my breath. I couldn't believe what had just happened. This was right. It was me.

A month or two later, I was on another meeting planning call when a colleague piped up to tell our field alignment director about the positive feedback from the mindfulness workshop at the national meeting, and it was requested that these types of workshops continue and that we should consider them becoming part of each live meeting we hold. I felt my heart leap. At all meetings to follow, I led early morning workshops that I called SoulFuel Workshops. Besides being so early, "mindfulness" and "connection" mean different things to different people, and let's be honest, we were at work, where talking about things like spiritual connection seems uncomfortable and maybe even a little taboo. But, if I was going to live my truth, then this was it. So I did. I didn't care if only one person was there, and I think for the first workshop this was exactly the case. But the number of people who show up keeps increasing, and who knows what will happen moving forward.

I say it all the time, I'm so honored to do this work. It's too important today. Not only do I want others to understand what it feels like to be connected, but I can't help but wonder how it might influence the way we communicate at work, how we show up, and most importantly, how we come together. I happen to believe that when a bunch of smart people bring their best selves to the table feeling free to share and wield their gifts, some serious magic happens. It is my intention to continue this work in my life, but also to teach it to leaders and how to bring it to their teams. I believe the result will be exactly what we should expect when we do anything in alignment with who we are, let alone a team of people doing it together – they will flourish.

I promise to report back as I am still very much in the testing phase in corporate America, but I know in my being it will change the game. The recipe I teach is this simple: truth, purpose, and power. Live your truth, lead with your heart, create space for love, and step into power….or better yet, let the magic happen, and it will. I dream of what can come from silenced egos and spiritual alignment in business, research and discovery, teaching, manufacturing, really in anything we are drawn to do as human beings in service to the betterment of the world. I believe the ideas we need now to change and save this world already exist within us. They simply lay dormant in fear because we are disconnected from ourselves and each other. I can't help but hear and wonder: *what would life look like if we awakened both?*

EXERCISE

1. Take a moment and think about how you are feeling right now. Write it down in your journal.

2. Now think about something you did that you know was good, that came from your heart, that you did in loving service for someone else.

3. In another part of the page in your journal, write down details, steps in the event, including the person you did this for and how they looked when you did what you did for them. Feel the moment as you write it.

4. Now sit in silence, clearing your mind and focusing only on what you wrote above. Visualize the moments you wrote down. Relive them.

5. Now think about how you feel and compare it to how you felt when you first started this exercise. Compare it to what you wrote when you first started this exercise.

Powerful, right?

TRANSFORMATION: A POEM

There is this place within you where she waits.

The one who is you is a place so familiar that when you go into her, you will know. She is a comfort that is home. Your eyes will swell with tears and every cell in your physical body will vibrate in a new way as you begin to understand what it means to be alive and alive with purpose.

It is you. True self.

And when you decide to love her, you become.

The power of this becoming unfolds before you gradually as she invites you to see and understand her little by little, as she shows you her power, one healed wound at a time.

She emerges slowly, gently, carefully.

She is aware she has wings now, though extra time will likely be needed for her to feel ready to use them. Yet the slow and purposeful emerging has created an awareness that they are there, different than before when she questioned if she could ever really have wings at all.

And then one day, perhaps unexpectedly, her wings open. The sun shines brightly and gloriously upon her, and she is undeniably whole and vibrant, powered by her truth.

All at once, she becomes aware of her beauty and power.

The wind, as if on cue, picks up and gently carries her to where she belonged all along.

She is flying now.

Bumpy, clumsy at first.

But she learns to ebb and flow with the wind, flowing with it instead of against it, yet owning her power.

Trusting it.

Trusting herself.

She soars.

Gracefully, confidently, purposefully.

The world cannot help but notice her now.

Look! Look! they will say.

Isn't she beautiful? Isn't she amazing?

How does she do it??

And then she lands.

Softly. Perfectly.

Taking in the sweet nectar of self-love, the power of transformation, and the never-ending magic of life and love that surround her. Then and always.

– Tammy L. Breznitsky

CHAPTER 6

TRANSFORMATION

"Our whole spiritual transformation brings us to the point where we realize in our own being, we are enough."
— Ram Dass

I have a very special niece. She is twelve years old and her name is Emery. She is not special just because she is my sister's child. She is special because she is connected to the world differently and her reality is predominantly ruled by her soul. Since she was a young child, she lived in and saw only the magic of the world. She engaged with it regularly, pulling on her powers naturally and freely. She was seen maybe as "different," a "dreamer" having a "strong and vivid imagination," but all I ever saw was a child whose soul was big, bold, and connected completely. All she was trying to do was to navigate her way through her Pandora. I can see it and understand her most of the time, but what is challenging for her is that living in her little human hybrid avatar, she is often confused with what she is told is truth and finds herself asking, without fully understanding that she is asking, "Where am I?"

She has a tremendous amount of support around her, especially in the form of my sister and her husband who help her cope, love her through it, and are doing an incredible job guiding her through this reality. Regardless, it is often difficult for them too, because it can be difficult for others to understand her and how she sees the world.

I'm writing some parts of this book over the Thanksgiving holiday and my sister was kind enough to host us this year. Emery took the liberty of creating a special gift for each of us in the form of little stories, accompanied by a drawing folded carefully on a piece of paper that was waiting for us on our plates when we sat down. She announced that the theme was "If so-and-so were an animal, he/she would be ..." or essentially a spirit animal analysis she conducted in her little world. The gift included a little note of why she was thankful for each of us. We went around the table and took turns reading them out loud before we ate. Each little snippet was perfectly matched to what she saw within that person in our family, and we all cheered, laughed, and clapped following each reveal. It was beautiful to watch each person light up while reading her words. All the while, she sat proudly and quietly at the end of the table, waiting anxiously for each person to open and receive the gift she'd created for them. She gives and receives with such grace, it's actually incredible to watch. She is an old, wise soul, and she is so naturally connected to her gifts which she wields without explanation or apology, standing proudly and bravely beside them.

My spirit animal was a butterfly.

Again, her insight is wiser than she knows.

The butterfly will forever remain maybe the most cliché, but still perfect example we have of true transformation and the magic of the world around us. You may have taken it for granted, but when you really take time to think about it, if you are not awed, you aren't really present.

When my son was younger, he was totally and completely obsessed with butterflies. We bought the butterfly kit online at least twice and spent an entire summer when he was eight years old collecting and researching butterflies. He was totally enamored by the butterfly kit and how amazing it was to open the little container of squirmy, brown, greenish yellow insects and then release them inside the netted home to crawl around, eat, and explore their little world. After a while, we would see their eating and activity slow down, and they began their journey to the roof of the encasement, where they would become still, welcoming the natural process of transformation to begin.

Eventually, we would wake to see the chrysalis hanging inside, and we observed how it was such a quiet scene. Still. Sacred, really. Then the only thing we could do from there on out was wait. The waiting was always the tough part. Each morning, he would race downstairs and into the sunroom to see if there was any activity or movement. Any signs of life emerging. The waiting might have felt like forever, but it was waiting with excited anticipation of what we knew was to come, knowing that a new being was about to emerge.

"How, mama? How does that happen?"

"Magic, Michael." I would say. "It's God's way of showing us His magic."

The butterfly life cycle is not only one to be amazed at, but is also one to carefully contemplate. The caterpillar doesn't just *change*. It doesn't come out of the cocoon as a new and different caterpillar. It is *transformed* into something *entirely new* and something quite beautiful. Understanding the nature of what is happening here is critical.

So what exactly is the difference between change and transformation?

The best definition I've ever read is from Chris McGoff from ThePrimes.com:

"Change requires becoming familiar with the current situation and working to make things better. The past is the fundamental reference point, and actions are intended to alter what already happened. When you choose change, the future is an improved version of the past.

Transformation is when we realize that the future can be described and realized only when you free yourself from constraints of the past. Transformation doesn't describe the future by referencing the past (better, faster, or cheaper); it births a future that is entirely new."

A butterfly is a *transformation*, not a *better* caterpillar.

You are not on this journey to become a *better* version of who you are now. You are about to *become* who you really are.

THE COCOON

Writing this book has been quite a transformative experience for me and part of my own personal emergence into my truth. I wrote the poem that opened this chapter earlier this year from inside my cocoon, feeling the need to express something during the agony of transformation. How does this transformation begin? How do you know when it is time to enter the cocoon? What does it feel like?

Prayer and meditation ultimately lead to an intense call inward. It is a calling for quiet solitude. It's the kind of intense calling that if somehow you could take a month off and buy a ticket to the middle of nowhere, you would do it in a heartbeat. It feels dark, weird, heavy, unsettling, yet you know there is something there you need.

Each time you visit with your soul in meditation during this time, you find she gently guides you deeper within yourself, where you are shown the way to the truth. She will guide you to your wounds, to your pain, and at first it will feel unbearable, but yet you notice that each time you sit with it, you find you begin to understand more and more of the truth. You will want to write it down and find it feels so good to do so. You might even speak it out loud when no one is around. It is the beginning.

She will show you things you need to see and hear, like how beautiful you really are, how strong you are, how far you've come, and how much you are loved. She will also show you things you don't want to see, like the root cause of those deep, painful, bleeding wounds that need deep healing and truths that you have spent your entire life pushing down or away. She will show you things you pretended weren't a big deal, but she knows how much those things have been festering, quietly but effectively eating away at you, blocking you from embracing her. She will show you how you are already forgiven and that now it is time to forgive yourself, and she will teach you how to love her in a way that will serve you the rest of your life.

She'll hold you through all of it – she is strong and powerful. She is Love, connected to unconditional Love. She too will tell you everything is going to be OK. Because it always will.

There will come a time in this darkness where you will realize that you are very uncomfortable, but you will simultaneously know that turning back is no longer an option, and honestly, it will feel terrifying. It feels all so unknown, so uncertain. You begin to see glimpses of what the new can look like. You will be introduced to the dreams weaved into your heart, and how those dreams directly complement your gifts. All of it will begin to feel surreal, and it will invigorate you. But even with those little glimpses, you'll still feel like it's all too much, all some kind of weird dream, and you will ask to wake up. But you won't. You can't. There will be days that you will believe you are officially crazy, and so you'll sprint back to what you think you know, anything to comfort you, but what you will find is that what you knew as normal and familiar is now only a source of frustration. You don't fit there. This is not who you are. You don't belong there anymore. But where do you belong?

You can't find what you are searching for because it isn't there yet; it's not in the old, *it is in the new being birthed through you.*

In the end, just like the butterfly, the result is soul-searingly beautiful, but the cocoon is pretty much a hot mess. It's just what you think it should be in there. That bumpy, crawly little green little bug has to dissolve to reform. It's mushy, soupy, messy, unstable, unformed, and unknown. But it cannot be rushed. It takes time and trust in the magic and the One who created you. Although you are beginning to understand that being directly linked to unconditional love, you are a co-creator of your new reality, for now *you know you must let go and let faith be your anchor.*

Even coming from a strong background of faith, I have found that the in-between is probably the most difficult part of this journey where I found I craved and begged to connect to other people who "get it." You realize that to get to the new, you desire new people and things in your life that help you move forward, not drag you backward. This can be the most difficult part, because shedding your skin also means shedding things and people that do not see what you are beginning to see. You will begin to look and act differently and realize that the language you are learning and using more regularly is not understood by others who once knew you well. They will say things like "Who are you? What's wrong with you? What happened to you?"

Because they don't speak this new language, the one you

are finding you prefer, they may decide they don't like this new you. They may decide they aren't interested in learning more about who you are becoming, and this is where letting go becomes a thing you must face. It's the rite of passage of this stage. I will not dance around the suffering that can exist here when you realize you have to let go of those people who aren't interested in the new you or in how to support this emerging new you. Much of the pain will be found when they will reveal themselves, and how, for the first time, you see them for who they truly are, you see the truth of their soul, whether you want to see it or not.

This is big work, my friends, and requires some deep connection, self-love practice, resilience, and trust in the process, and as I mentioned early, having a good spiritual life coach is often a great idea to support you through this phase. I had to seek and invest in my own life coach and support team during this time and it was a game changer.

FORMING

The importance of a strong meditation and prayer practice, along with journaling of what you are feeling, hearing, and seeing during this time, cannot be overstated. You have to really agree to meet your soul where she is, listen to her, and most importantly, act on what she tells you. This sounds simple, but like anything, it takes time to trust that what you are hearing and feeling is real. This can't all be kept in your head and heart. The cocoon is a time for quiet inward healing, but the actual transformation takes work out in the world. Of course, God works His part of the magic like He will always do, but you must have skin in the game, which itself takes bravery. It takes willingness to keep moving forward, to begin to live the truth of what you know is right for you, even in the midst of what feels like massive uncertainty and most people who thought they knew you telling you otherwise. It's having wobbly legs and a shaky voice but choosing to stand up and speak anyway. It is carrying on in the midst of loneliness as people who you thought loved you are peeled away.

It also takes courage. Courage is not acting in the absence of fear – it is feeling fear and acting anyway. The only way to find the way is to try it on, see if it feels right, probably screw up (which is going to happen whether you want it to or not), and be willing to keep going in spite of it all. You have to trust yourself enough to believe that whatever you find or run into, you will figure it out. Believe that you are supported to do so.

When we let the soul run the show for a while, we become aware of the magic of our transformation. The ego will fight you, rolling its eyes saying, "Just wait and see, you are going to pay for this," which will feel terrible. Until you remember that you aren't paying for anything. You are connected, and everything is going exactly as it should. This is the time when our connection to infinite wisdom and unconditional Love is grown and strengthened by us choosing to let the magic happen.

You will find that the more you connect, the more you are

learning to let go of what you think you want and need. You will find it easier to instead ask the soul to bring you what it knows you need, and then go and do whatever it is. The best part is that, in seemingly perfect timing, you will find those new sources of energy and love waiting for you, and they will carry you. They will likely surprise you, showing up when you least expect them to, but when you needed them to. You will find that you don't just enjoy these new things, but you are part of them. You are one with them. New people will enter your life, and it will feel like you've known them forever. New experiences will be opened and made available to you through them and to them through you.

Finally, one glorious day, you will realize that there is indeed potent magic in this period of transformation. You realize that you haven't been dissolved at all – only the things that weren't real were dissolved, and now you stand naked. Naked and oh so incredibly vulnerable, which is also the most powerful you've ever been.

EMERGENCE

Soon you will see glimpses of the new you again, but now they will begin to take shape and become real possibilities. Is that a flicker of light? Yes. Indeed it is. You are inching closer and closer, getting more confident as the flicker grows brighter, bigger, and finally cracks open into something you could never have expected. You are on your way now, until all at once, you find you are free.

What does it mean to be free? It means freeing yourself from the chains of what other people think you should be doing to doing what your heart tells you to do. It comes from doing the work in the cocoon to transform, to face the pain, face the truth, and to emerge new and whole, albeit with wet wings, and then be brave enough to be patient while they dry. Everyone you know will be gawking and staring, and you will be thinking, OK, great, now what? And then you will realize that you know not only what to do, but exactly *what you want to do.* And now it's time to go do it.

When I gave myself permission to speak my heart at that first workshop, I promise you my wings were very new and very wet, but by doing so, I gave myself a taste of freedom, and I believe it changed the trajectory of my life and career forever. What do you think it will look like for you when you emerge from your cocoon? Maybe write a journal passage from your heart and see what comes up. Or better yet, maybe it's time you found out.

CHAPTER 7

AWAKENING AND ACTIVATION

"Intuition is a very powerful thing, more powerful than intellect."
— Steve Jobs

E mergence from the cocoon is nothing short of exhilarating. It's the equivalent of riding your banshee in Pandora for the first time. You realize that you are seeing new things that you have never seen before because you've never been able to fly this way before. You are connected, confident, in control, and unapologetic. The sun is shining on you, and there is awareness of a natural hum, a melody that all of life on earth is synched to, and for the first time ever, you realize that you are part of that hum and it would never sound same if you did not do the work to emerge and contribute your energy to it.

You *hear* things differently.

You *see* things differently.

You *know* things differently.

You are filled with undeniable awe, wonder, and most importantly, recognition and understanding that you are not only part of it, but you are *one with it.*

Because of this new awareness, you are able to see something you have never seen before – *you see you.*

She is beautiful.

She is glowing.

She is strong.

She is lit from the inside out.

She is Love and loved unconditionally simultaneously.

You realize that fear does not and cannot exist here. It is nothing more than an illusion of epic proportions. It holds no power. It only had power *because you gave it power.* All of the power came from you. You look at the cocoon you emerged from and realize the magic that just happened is happening all around you. You know now that you came from the source of all things, and you are always and infinitely connected to it. There is no fear when there is truth, and you know the truth is you were made in the image of God. Truth and *Love* control your avatar. You have work to do on Love's behalf, and you know you are called to do it just by the fact that you exist.

In spirituality, this moment is called a*wakening,* and it is something that, when it happens, you never forget it. It is the moment when you stop agonizing over your purpose. You understand that just being alive is fulfilling your purpose, and your next vocation is on its way to you.

You also become aware of gifts that you have always had, but are now primed and readily accessible for you as you explore this new world. It's like discovering your avatar has amazing superpowers that are now ready to be *activated.*

Let's take them one by one.

THE POWER OF BELIEF

Having faith is one thing, and we talk about it often, but one aspect of faith I think sometimes gets lost is the power it gives us. It needs to brought to the forefront more readily and more often. Let's discuss.

Have you ever considered that fear and faith have one major thing in common: they both ask us to believe in something we cannot see? Think about it. Neither is concrete or material, but both vie for our attention and have the power to pull us in completely different directions leading to very different outcomes, right? This is yet another point reflecting the nature of our innate spirituality and power. What our hearts decide is truth is what we see and ultimately what we experience, since the energy of the universe follows our command. You choose fear, you get fear and everything that comes with it – lack, frustration, anger, envy, and suffering. Choose faith, you get truth, love, hope, trust, and genuine happiness. Fear is powerful and available only when there is a lack of faith, not the other way around. Faith is innate to connection and true self-love. Fear is illusion and ushered in only when we lack faith.

When we have faith and believe, we are empowered in a different way. We can act differently because we know everything is exactly as it should be and that something bigger than us, something that knows us and loves us is in control and has our backs. I can think of many times, especially lately with writing this book, faced with conflicting calendars, and endless to-do lists where I said, "Well, this is going to get interesting, but I know it's taken care of. I know something will come up to make it work out." So, I let it go. And guess what? It did. Every. Single. Time.

There are many books written on belief, including those published about the science and research around the kind of power that resides in people who have faith and how it allows them to live out their purpose differently. From the classics like *The Magic of Belief* by Claude Bristol or *The Power of Belief* by Bruce Lipton, to the last chapter in Marie Forelo's book, *Everything Is Figureoutable,* there are many examples of this kind of work and the people who know and understand the power it holds. But it was the simplicity of Jen Sincero's words that made it click for me. She is one of my favorite authors because her authentic voice and effortless wit keep me wanting more. I'm pretty sure she and I would be good friends. Anyway, she wrote that you have to believe it like it's already a done deal, and then let go and wait for it to arrive. I found that the best thing you can do is not only let go, but expect to be surprised at what you get.

My lake house is a good example of this. We keep our boat on a lake in the Poconos and have vacationed there for a number of summers. Mike and I decided we wanted to invest in finding a home there for our family. We looked for a number of years, but even when we found something we liked, it seemed to fall through. Two separate houses we bid on went all the way to inspection, where they failed miserably. Mike had given up, but not me.

Another winter came and went and I brought it up to him again, but this time, it was different. I knew I was going to write this book, and I needed a quiet place where I could write and create. This time, I was a different kind of serious, and it was to serve a different kind of purpose. I wanted a place that was mine, a place that naturally created that sacred connection I told you about in previous chapters. I knew it was out there. I envisioned what it would look like, what it would feel like, how I would decorate it. I realized before, I was playing small. I didn't really believe we would find our house, and I didn't really want the houses we put bids on, because the truth was that deep in my heart, I wanted it to be lakefront.

I wanted to wake up with the water to pull on its peace and energy. I decided now I was going to find it. Mike thought I was bonkers, so he let me go crazy. He never thought we could afford a lakefront house. I ignored him. I cut out pictures of what felt right to me and I hung them on a corkboard. I bought decorations (for a house that wasn't mine yet) that I found in stores when I was shopping. I daydreamed about gifting it to friends and family as a place to recharge and reconnect. I began to look at houses on the websites we were familiar with that were selling houses on the lake we were interested in and had been looking on, but I expanded my reach, changed realtors, and believed we would have it by the end of the coming summer.

One day in early June, I was scrolling through a few houses, and one made me pause. It wasn't on the lake we were looking on, but it was close enough, about twenty-five minutes from where we keep our boat. This home was adorable, small and quaint, in a nature preserve and on a much smaller but beautifully maintained lake and quiet community. It was lakefront and a little outside of our price range, but I knew we had to go see it.

I called the realtor and set up a viewing for this and a few other houses that seemed worth our time. It was the first house we looked at that day, but long story short, we drove down the road to the community, I took one look at the lake and I felt my heart leap. We drove slowly up to the property where it seemed to welcome us, all shiny and bright in the sun, the brown wood contrasting so beautifully against the green ferns that lined the way. I stepped one foot into the house, saw the beams line the roof, saw the view of the lake with the property leading down to it, and I knew this was it. I knew Mike knew it too.

We took the boat out that afternoon to talk about the houses we saw and Mike said to me, "Tammy, I want that house for you and for us, but I don't know how we will find the money. Can we afford it?" Here's where faith is everything. I told him not to worry. If we both feel it, we should go for it. We did.

Here's what happened: the realtor chose our bid, came down in price, the little extra money we needed came through stocks we owned that rose just in time, to the point where the *exact* amount we needed down was exactly what we had. We closed and moved in that August.

I realized one day sitting on that lake that I have been doing this my whole life. It is exactly how I have what I have and is exactly how I'm going where I'm going. You don't need anything more than what you already have to manifest whatever you want, and as long as it is in your best interests and is asked for with good intention to serve others, it's yours. I walk around all the time offering things up to God and just letting Him do the magic to make it work. I flow, follow what is put in front of me, trust what I hear and what comes through, and trust the plan. Make no mistake. What you believe is what you co-create with Source, and what you want to co-create is entirely up to you.

Fear or faith. Every day, every decision, every moment, we get a choice. Believe, trust, let go, and act like it's already yours, even when you hit blocks. Believe it's going to work out. Reflect, connect, re-route if you need to, but keep going and believing, and it will be exactly when it is supposed to be for your highest and greatest good. *This is the power of belief.*

THE POWER OF GRATITUDE

I believe we significantly underestimate and do not fully comprehend how much God loves us. But one thing is for sure – in order to live the magical life we all dream of that was intended for us, *we have to return that love and trust completely through having unshakeable faith,* which should be followed with gratitude and connection. Especially when life gets really tough, which it will. Gratitude is our second greatest superpower.

Being amazed at life and the world we live in should invoke gratitude, whether it is following your awakening or when your faith pulls you through or shows up as an answered prayer we needed. An incredible amount of work has been done documenting the power *gratitude* has in our lives. That being said, I think we tend to associate gratitude with feeling happy and good. While it is indeed very powerful and very important to turn to in times of happiness, where we go wrong is that we tend to devalue its power when we are suffering.

Let's be honest. We are still on our Pandora, we have a lot to learn, and there will be suffering. Turning to gratitude is our armor, a buffer to the hit our hearts may be taking. When we turn to being present to what is in front of us in times of suffering and feel grateful and express gratitude, it causes a shift in emotional energy away from the negative and re-focuses our minds on the things that truly matter – the blessings we already have.

It serves to remind us that we are always loved and everything is exactly as it is supposed to be. It centers us. It raises our awareness that what we have *right now is exactly what we need*. The past cannot be changed. The future is unknown, but when we choose to focus on the blessings we *do* have, we become present, and it naturally brings us back to one thing: Love. Being present, especially in gratitude, invokes organic connection and prayer leading to meditation because we are naturally and organically sent inward, whether it is to express love or to reach for Love asking for the answer or the strength we need to continue. So, how can we be present and show up in gratitude? This brings us right back to the means of connection – prayer and meditation.

Before I get out of bed every morning, I take a moment to be aware of being conscious, and I think about how I feel about what I know is going on that day. Then I immediately shift my thoughts to three things I have to be grateful for right now. I visualize them, feel them, and let that feel flood my heart and spread over me entirely. It's changed everything for me, because I know that, regardless of what happens that day, I know what I already have, and what I already have is very, very good.

Then I meditate.

Meditation is a form of prayer, but here is the difference: in prayer, you are *talking* to God, in meditation, you are *listening*. It is when you decide to listen that you realize what you need to hear comes through. It directly informs and prepares you for your day. Your feet hit the floor feeling like you know exactly what you should do, and if it doesn't go as you hoped it would, it's OK, because you know you are loved, and everything always is.

If lying in bed to pray isn't your thing, prayer and meditating doesn't have to be a chunk of time or a huge to-do. You can begin as simply as ensuring ten minutes of quiet time over your coffee in the morning. Get out of bed ten minutes earlier so you can make that quiet time happen. Choose to clear your head so you can begin to listen to your heart. Begin with gratitude for everything you have, and then just allow the silence to fold over you. You might be surprised at what you hear. Write it down. Know it takes practice to quiet your mind, so go easy on yourself. Keep trying and if you are really stuck, ask for quiet and clarity, and it will be given to you. Remember, this is an innate power, so you already know how to do it. You have to show up with the intent to learn, keep trying, and believing it is something you know how to do. Remember, both fear and meditation are like a muscle – the more you use it, the stronger it gets. The same is true of fear and faith. Choose wisely.

THE POWER OF INTUITION: OUR SPIRITUAL SUPER POWER

The final and most important superpower is the power of intuition. Intuition is often referred to as our "sixth sense" or "gut feeling." It's knowing something without reason. I believe our intuition is the gift that evolves out of working that muscle of faith and connection. It is our lifeline when we need it most, and it communicates directly from our subconscious soul to our consciousness without giving our minds the opportunity to reason. It's truth before we get to decide whether or not it makes sense, and in many situations, the answer will not make sense. We somehow "just know" it's what we must do.

Being an intuitive empath, I love this one. It's my strongest and most potent spiritual gift, the one I use without knowing I'm using it; it's my thing. I'm confident you've experienced and used yours before too. Everyone has access to their intuition always. It's that something telling you not to eat that yogurt or drive into the city, but to catch the train instead. It is a very, very powerful gift, and once we learn to really discern its voice from the one of your mind, it serves as your guiding light in every possible situation. I will tell you, this is a gift to get pretty darn excited about. It has freaked me out, amazed me, and frankly, saved me more than I want to admit. Like anything new, it is something you will need to practice and listen for carefully, but when you get it, you get it, and nothing is ever the same.

If you feel like this is relatively new to you, or that you wish to learn to engage it more, you can absolutely learn to tap into it. Can you take a guess at how? Yup. Meditate. Connect. Listen. Write down what you hear. Then begin to trust it and act on what you hear. This is one of those things you have to experience for yourself, and the way to do it is to act on what you think you hear and see what happens. I promise you, you will be amazed.

You are powerful. A very powerful human avatar indeed.

Believe it.

Then honor it by letting the life you live be an example of how much you do.

JOURNAL EXERCISE

- Find some quiet time and to begin by taking three deep breaths. Allow yourself to connect to your breath and the silence around you. Sink into it and let it wash over you. Just breathe. Don't force it. Allow your mind to call on three things you are grateful for. Let me get you started with some examples: kids, pets, legs that work, a heart that beats, car that drives, job that pays the bills. Write them down on the paper or in your journal.

- Each morning, begin your day with this prayer before you get out of bed:

  "*Thank you, Love/God/Source for the gift of this life. I am so grateful for…*" Then, "*I need you now. I need you to help clear my head and allow me to hear you.*"

- Write down what you hear in your journal.

- Decide each day, or once a week, to act on one thing you find yourself saying you should do, or "feeling" like you should do, regardless if it makes sense to your brain or not. Choose to do it.

- Write down what it is, and write down what you found.

- Repeat for two weeks and see what happens!

A PERFECT, REAL LIFE EXAMPLE

Human brains tend to connect to and remember things when they are told through a good story. I don't think there is a more perfect example of these superpowers we just discussed being used so effectively than what we learn when we examine the story of Jesus' life. Regardless of what you believe or how you identify religiously, stick with me here because it's worth it, I promise.

From all the other "ascended masters," Jesus' story is unique to me because it feels so relatable. In the church, we tend to get so focused on the fact that, ultimately, He was the Son of God (which He was, but for the record, most of the humans living around at that time didn't even figure *that* out until after we killed Him) that we forget one important, and to me, the most *critical* part of the story:

He was human, too. And If we are going to walk around claiming to be connected to an infinite Source and say we are made in God's likeness, then it's time we owned it.

Let's start at the beginning. Although the focus of Christmas is on the birth of Jesus, I find I am always drawn to Mary and Joseph when I think about this story. I've spent time meditating on what it must have felt like to be living what they chose to live through. There had to be some serious confusion, a good dose of fear, and many gut-wrenching, sleepless nights. Frankly, they were suffering. A lot. Yet, in spite of it all, they said yes. Yes to the crazy. Yes to the impossible. Yes to God, even though it was all super weird and outside their ability to reason or understand. I find it interesting to think of it this way.

From Mary's perspective, one minute, you're a woman doing your thing. The next, you are visited by an angel telling you that you have favor with God and boom, you're miraculously pregnant. Your boyfriend ditches you when he learns you're pregnant. You can't tell him the story because the angel told you not to, so you let it be and wonder what the heck is going to happen next.

For Joseph, his head is spinning, and his heart is broken when he learns Mary is pregnant, so he falls asleep in grief only to dream of an angel who tells him not to fear because his girl-friend is carrying God's son. Joseph wakes up from his dream and chooses to believe what he heard and returns to Mary. Of course he had a choice. He chose to listen to his intuition and his heart, and he chose Mary; he chose God's plan.

But let's talk about crazy...one minute, he's marrying a virgin, the next he's marrying a pregnant virgin. Let *that* sink in for a minute. He had to have some serious faith, love, and trust to follow through. In fact, they both chose trust. They were shunned by the people who loved them, and they did what they were asked regardless. And that takes some serious guts.

Fast-forward nine months or so later. You are Mary, on a donkey, now in a foreign town. You can't find a place to sleep, you are in labor, and the best God is doing for you is putting you in a barn. You are lying in some hay with a whole bunch of smelly animals around you, about to have a baby, thinking, "Well, great God, this is awesome."

And then, imagine holding that baby... like *what*?

Imagine poor Joseph, who had to be in total, utter, profound bewilderment. He was probably trying to figure out if this was all real, and then it just keeps on getting crazier. Suddenly, you have visitors out of nowhere – shepherds who heard of the birth from angels, followed by a caravan of three kings from foreign lands, kneeling before you and this baby, offering gifts and love. The baby you are responsible for taking care of that was born out of nothing. You know, God's son. No biggie.

I know it's all holy, but come on. They had to be saying *holy crap*. I know for sure that's what I'd be saying. But that is my favorite part. Once it was all said and done, what did they get for believing, for trusting, for using their intuition to follow through the crazy and just sticking it all out?

Wonderment.

Awe.

Peace.

Hope.

Indescribable and life-altering joy.

Legacy. Their story is has been told generation after generation since their existence.

And then there is the gift of Christmas in Jesus.

I repeat relatively often throughout this book that you are loved. How much are you loved? *You are loved so much so that God, through Jesus and His life, showed us that the power of the universe can and does fit perfectly into our humanity.*

The power of the Universe is inside you. And if that isn't powerful, I don't know what is.

But let's keep going and dig a little deeper because there is so much more. One of the things most people know about Jesus was that He walked around doing good things, including curing people, healing people, and literally bringing them back from the dead. The most powerful part of this meditation for me was when I realized that there is one common thread throughout all of these miracles documented in the bible. It is one key statement that exists in some form or another that

Jesus proclaims after almost every act of healing: He lays His hands on the person, but then gently reminds them that that they had skin in the game.

"... go now, your faith has healed you ...
your faith has made you well ... "
— Mark 5:34, Luke 17:11-19, Mark 10:52,
Luke 8:48, Luke 7:50 NIV

Your faith has healed you.

In other words, you have a big part in healing yourself. It begins and ends with faith. The power of believing will heal you by guiding you how to love yourself.

This is exactly why my faith is and always has been the cornerstone of my life. There is so much worth claiming it for, and once you get a taste of it, including bringing it with you into your daily life, including to work and how you view work, everything changes. This story and countless others have been documented for our good, to reaffirm our belief regardless of what we think we see, to invoke gratitude and to give us the courage to trust the power of our intuition.

When I decided I wanted to get to know Jesus differently than just what I was told in school, here is what drew me to Him the most: He grew up, just like you and me. He gets it; He gets this world in every way possible. He was here. He was human. He knows how I feel and He knows how you feel. How can I say that? What do I mean? Some great examples:

He got yelled at by his parents for wandering away.

He was there with His mother and grieved when his earthly father died.

He had to have His mother give him a kick in the butt when it was time to take on his life's work, stop drinking the wine at a wedding, and instead make some.

He knows what it is like to be hungry.

He knows what it is like to be lonely.

He knows and experienced the power of temptation when He was hungry and lonely in the desert.

He knows what it is like to have to go to work to teach and feed other human beings, even when it seemed impossible to do. He even had to go out on a boat to get away from these people.

He knows what it feels like to be angry and literally want to throw some tables. Because He did.

He knows what it is like to see people suffer. But He also knows the pure joy of seeing people's faith come alive to heal themselves.

He showed us how to be patient with and love the people who are lost, who don't believe in God, or who believe in other gods.

He knows the degree of evil that exists in this world on every single level.

He was betrayed by one of His best friends tempted by that evil.

He was ultimately tortured by the people He healed and cured and taught and loved.

He knows how needy we are. He knows how mean we can be. He knows the weakness within us. He knows the weakness of our simple minds and how we can easily be swayed by others or what we think we know.

He knows the depth of suffering we are capable of inflicting on others.

And He showed us what it truly means to love one another. Because in spite of it all, He loved all those people anyway. Right down to the very last moments of His life while suffering on the cross. Just like He loves me and you in spite of ourselves.

He also showed us how to love the righteous people who think they know God, even though they couldn't see they were staring God's son right in the face. He continues to love those who still exist today.

His humanity shines when I hear the story of how He prayed for the cup to pass Him during his agony in the garden. He knew what was coming. He knew the suffering that He was to endure, and He was human and He was freaking terrified.

But because he loves us, because He knows His father and knows His power, He chose God's will and, in turn, showed us what it means to surrender. Completely.

He knows joy. He knows pain. He knows suffering.

So I turn to Him and I trust Him because I can't do any of this work without Him. It would be pointless to try. This is why the Jesus I know is my best friend forever, my guy on meditation speed dial, the voice in my heart, the One who walks with me and helps me see and understand myself and other people. He is always guiding me home – home to my heart where I rediscovered my love for spirituality. He has guided me to other religions and the meaning of what spirituality is for other people so I can learn and love them better. Knowing Jesus the way I do is the greatest gift of my life, and it was time that I share this guy I know with you and the world. Following my awakening, I knew I was being called to share Him this way, especially outside of a church, religion, and institutional faith, especially to those who don't know Him at all. By the way, He knows all about the politics and intricacies of how our egos basically screw up spirituality. *We tortured and mocked and crucified Him for a new opinion of what God and spirituality really mean, remember?*

He's easy. He's funny. I'm serious. Just like any other best friend you might have, all He really wants from you is the gift of you. The real you. The *you* His Father, Source of all, creator of the Universe, *the* universe, created. To me, He is the ultimate example of what it looks like to show up as who you are to use your gifts and do what you are here to do. All while doing so, you're trusting God's plan for your life, right down to the minute your time on earth is over and we leave our avatar, just as He left His.

So do you see a common thread here? Do you see how it all comes together?

We have to connect with our true self to unearth and fall in love with our truth and transform into it. Living your truth requires consistent connection to Love, which ignites faith or belief, which manifests our dreams. Belief is reaffirmed by practicing gratitude, especially in the face of suffering, which reminds us of the blessings we asked for that we already have, which brings us back to trust—trusting ourselves and our connection to the truth that comes to us and is lived through us. All of it comes together through prayer and meditation and connection to entities like Jesus who get it, who see us, who love us and support us in doing the work we are asked to do with full hearts. All we have to have is the willingness to flow and trust God's plan and to surrender to it.

CHAPTER 8

YOUR SOUL ON FIRE

"See the girl with the diamonds and the shoes?
She walks around like she's got nothin' to lose
Yes she's a go-getter, she's everybody's type
She's a queen of the city but she don't believe the hype
She's got her own elevation, holy motivation
Till I wrote some letters on big bold signs
I got faith in you baby, I got faith in you now
And you've been such a, such a good friend of me
Know that I love you somehow
I met you, hallelujah, I got faith"
– Adapted from the song "Faith" and the movie
Sing by Stevie Wonder

I s there any song by Stevie Wonder that does *not* make you feel good? Anyway, let's review what we've learned about this journey so far:

- Being uncomfortable in the face of what you thought were your plans is usually our prompt that it is time to seek out true vocation.

- The path to finding that vocation comes through connection and building a relationship with something bigger than ourselves, balancing out ego, and allowing our soul to come forward.

- Once we are connected to our soul and agree to get to know her, we begin the process of transformation and healing our hearts to give us courage to become who we truly are.

- Once complete, we emerge from the in-between with an awakened heart, connected to the truth and to the power of our spiritual being, who we understand now is infinitely connected to the power of Love. This gives us the confidence to seek out our vocation in a new way, knowing and trusting that we are always guided and unconditionally loved.

Now the *real work* begins. But before we go there, let's pause and acknowledge how far you've come. Getting through those above steps takes an incredible amount of work and courage. We are often in such a hurry to get to the next thing that we miss the joy of the now, and really, it's all we have. This was such an important realization following awakening for me. Setting goals for what you thought would make you happy five years from now does nothing more than have you missing your life and the magic within it. Stress and pressure take over and life becomes an endless list of to-dos. Instead, I chose to slow down, be in the moment, and be grateful for all I have now, what I have the privilege of doing, *not what I thought I need.* It was truly a game-changer. Celebrating how far you've come ensures you are taking a moment to be present, reflecting, powering up gratitude, connecting, and fully celebrating it every step of the way.

Here we are now, at the final step in discovering what is next and exactly what to do next. Of course, finding the answer will require work, but that work should be fun, effortless, enjoyable, and exciting, not confusing, frustrating, difficult, painful, or backbreaking.

If we believe the world is orchestrated by the undeniable force of Love, then our job is quite simple. We connect to it, let God's plan flow to us and through us, knowing it is unfolding perfectly. Once again, as human avatars with egos who try to bully us, we tend to overanalyze and overcomplicate this part, but the truth is that the answers are right in front of us. They always have been. We've just been asleep, distracted, or a little bit of both. Our lives lived up to our awakening hold all the clues we need, and now, awake, connected to, and *in love* with our true selves, we get to write a different story with a different kind of confidence.

Think of Emma in *The Key to the Extraordinary* – do you see now that your Destiny Dream has already happened? *You just woke up from it.*

This is where the Three Golden Keys of spirituality – *connection, reflection, and service,* shared so brilliantly with us by William Bloom – lay the foundation of the triad to wholeness and a life of vocation. Hopefully, I've driven home the critical importance of connection throughout this book, but let's dive more into the other two components so we can fully understand how these three keys will allow you to discern the clues to your destiny dream and send you on your way to living a life of purpose.

REFLECTION FOLLOWING TRANSFORMATION

According to William Bloom in *The New Spirituality*, reflection is summed up as the following:

"[Reflection is] the ability look at ourselves and willingness to learn more about who we really are, the nature of our character, and psychology, our purpose, and our real essence. The ability to observe, inquire into, and contemplate ourselves, our thoughts, our emotions, and our instincts and play back memories and impressions locked within the subconscious, meeting them, endeavoring to understand, accept, and integrate them, and anticipate our future and how our past may influence it, and use our higher consciousness, our mind, to observe, review, examine, and judge our thoughts and behavior, contemplating the higher order of nature listening to the inner voice of our wiser self, not blame others but understand that we can create our own lives and consciously change ourselves and keep an open mind."

What he is saying is that reflection is critical because the ability to step outside of ourselves and review life we lived to date allows us to see a bigger picture, and moving forward, "watch" our life unfold before us. We begin to see patterns and truths of who we have always been. Within those truths lie the clues to our purpose. We understand that we are playing them back not to be critical and degrade ourselves for making stupid mistakes, but to understand, accept why we did what we did, what happened as a result of those actions, and most importantly, what we learned from them. This allows us to predict what we might do if and when that situation arises again.

We can evaluate these mistakes with love because we know we are loved regardless. We are loved unconditionally. Lastly, now fully connected with our soul and having faith in its infinite connection to Love, we can tap into that inner voice, and with an open mind and heart, call on and trust our intuition. Then, we begin to create the life we were put here to live.

UNMASKING AND TAKING BACK YOUR POWER

Faith and fear cannot exist together, so our soul and connection to Love naturally unmasks our fears, puts them on the table for us to see in plain sight, and shows us why they are there in the first place. We see that they existed only because we lacked faith and connection, but now you know who you are and from where you came. This allows you to take back your power. When we take back our power, fear dissolves before our eyes. This is what is meant by "fear is an illusion." Once we see our fears for what they really are, we realize they hold no power. There is no need for ego to protect us from the storms of life. You control the storm. *You hold the power within you.* You always have.

When our truth becomes part of us, when we receive it and let it sink into our hearts, we realize we are no longer interested in what other people think about us and the path we choose to take. We are only interested in one thing: living the life we are here to live. You will find that you can do so unapologetically. This isn't just a five-year plan that you have to create and follow, seeking approval and validation from others. This isn't *your* plan to success, *it's God's plan.* So, we can happily, cheerfully, and effortlessly go about enjoying our life, being fully present, and working hard creating that life in full alignment to our purpose. We can believe everything is going to fall into place exactly as it should at exactly the right time, and it always will. People will say things like, *"How does she always seem to know the way, see the big picture, or know where to go to find the next thing that always seems to take off for her? She's so lucky."*

You're not lucky. You're just awake and connected.

Choosing to live a life aligned to purpose breaks open the channel to seemingly infinite energy, joy, and happiness, regardless of your circumstances. You know the type: someone who seems to be happy all the time, or who seems to have this endless source of energy or "bubbliness," regardless of the circumstances they are in. These people may be described as *annoyingly happy,* or *really energetic or passionate*...or they seem to have this incredible level of resilience like, *man she took a hit but bounced back quite well.* These people are happy to own every single minute. They tend to see the bright side of everything and always have this knack for finding or seeing the silver lining. They enjoy helping other people see it too. They can do this because they know that mistakes are not failures and suffering is not punishment. Mistakes hold the gift of learning and suffering is only an opportunity to grow more in love with Love.

This is how we become magnets for greatness and abundance and how we gain influence and credibility. It's how we become leaders in a world desperate for the kind of leadership that takes us where every single human being alive is dying to be—home to themselves. The effect of this leadership results in you hearing people say, *"I want to be with her. I want to be around her, with her, on her team. I will fight alongside her"* because they know you have that "thing." Something maybe they can't explain, but they do know that they just feel better or happier being around you and feel uplifted overall when they leave you. They trust you. They believe in you. So they work harder willingly. Not because they want to impress you, but because they know they can show up as their authentic selves, and something about that feels different and right. You are giving them permission for their true self, their soul, to step forward, maybe triggering their own invitation to transformation.

You and I know that "thing" they can't put their finger on is nothing more than *Love.*

Love naturally and organically shines through people connected to their truth and onto people around them. This is what I mean when I said *we are living our purpose just by being alive.* How? Because Love in people, still asleep or awake, recognizes itself. The spiritual part of that person identifies itself in the other, and their souls recognize each other. They are connected because we are all connected. We are infinitely connected to that from which we came – Love, God, the Holy Spirit, and Jesus who embodied Love on earth, just like you and I do right now.

There is a prayer that Mother Teresa loved that I say every morning, but especially when I am going into an important meeting or event. I want to share it with you because I have found it is very powerful. My soul immediately responds and shines when I hear it. I know yours will too:

Dear Jesus, help me to spread Your fragrance everywhere I go.
Flood my soul with Your spirit and life.
Penetrate and possess my whole being so utterly,
That my life may only be a radiance of Yours.
Shine through me, and be so in me
That every soul I come in contact with
May feel Your presence in my soul.
Let them look up and see no longer me, but only Jesus.
Stay with me and then I shall begin to shine as You shine,
So to shine as to be a light to others;

The light, O Jesus will be all from You; none of it will be mine;
It will be you, shining on others through me.
Let me thus praise You the way You love best,
by shining on those around me.
Let me preach You without preaching, not by words but
by my example,
By the catching force of the sympathetic influence of what I do,
The evident fullness of the love my heart bears to You.

Amen.

FINDING YOUR PURPOSE AND STEPPING INTO YOUR POWER

So, now you may be thinking, this is great and all, but *how* exactly do I know my purpose? How do I find my vocation? How will I know when I found it?

It is as simple as linking the outputs of our connection and reflection exercises to unearth and reconnect with our gifts and choose to use them to serve others.

Every soul has been gifted with unique, individual gifts to fulfill its purpose on earth. Those gifts are present within our human avatar from the minute we are born into it. Our gifts become evident from a young age when we are naturally drawn to certain things, and most of the time, doing those things is pretty effortless. When I began my search for my purpose, I looked back at my life and figured out pretty quickly some pretty glaringly obvious gifts and truths.

I always had a deep and intimate connection with my spirit and with God, even as a child. I was constantly praying and found myself in adoration and quiet meditation regularly. I shared with you previously that, in college, I discerned a vocation to become a nun, but was shown very clearly that my soul called for me to be a mother. Throughout my life, I had a number of spiritual experiences that allowed for a deep sense of knowing things without knowing how I know them. I am highly empathic and intuitive. Before my awakening, I knew these things happened to me, but I was literally terrified of them. They freaked me out, they freaked people close to me out. So I just let them alone for the most part. I dabbled with them, called on them when I really needed to, but that was it. I was more focused on proving to everyone that I was going to not only survive my childhood, but I was going to rise above it and be as successful as possible.

I also noted that I was a gifted speaker and could easily connect to and engage an audience. Writing papers from high school through college was easy for me, and honestly enjoyable. I even wrote my boyfriend's papers. I found people looked to me for advice and maybe could sense my intuition around things. When I was in a high vibration state, I learned I could predict random events, like where an arrow might fall on a wheel at a fair by projecting my energy from my gut to guide me to where it will land. I did this quite effectively this summer with my son, and he is totally convinced I have "special powers," which totally cracks me up, because he does too. So does my daughter. They just have to learn how to harness them.

I think you see where this is going. I'm here writing this book and decided to devote the next part of my life as a speaker and spiritual life coach for one reason – because my story, my gifts and my soul have led me here. To you. To share my gifts with you and to be part of helping people reconnect to their souls, to Love, so Love can change hearts, guide them to purpose, and we can begin to change the world, creating heaven on earth, one person at a time.

What I can't help but think about is what the world would be like if we taught this to our children from a young age. What if we removed all of the exceptions from them and their future and just asked them to navigate their lives following the compass of joy and happiness? What if we taught them that not only was this acceptable, but it was sacred and was the only way to tap into true abundance – that doing the thing that lit them up in turn lights up the world, and the world repays with giving us everything we need and then some? What if we taught them that the things that make us joyful and happy are derived from a natural connection to our souls and, hence, leave very little room for fear to rear its ugly head. If we were to do this, we just might raise a generation of people who change the face of humanity forever.

My son, like my niece Emery, is an old soul. I smile when I write that, as he and Emery were born only five days apart. I say it all the time when I talk about him, but his soul is visible in his eyes, and he draws you right into it, almost like you fall into a trance of sorts. I saw and felt it the minute they placed him in my arms. He has a presence, charisma, and a way with words which creates a great deal of influence that he is well aware of and that he learned quickly how to use to his advantage.

A great example of this is my favorite story from when he was in second grade. One night at dinner, he announced he wanted to play football. We listened and then pretty much said he was too young and there wasn't a team outside of flag football that we would be comfortable with him playing in. He said, *"OK, well I'll create my own team to play in the yard."* And my husband Mike and I were like, "OK, great," thinking he would find some buddies for a pick-up game. Well. He went to school the next day and convinced his friends that they could start a football team that my husband would coach. He convinced the girls they could be cheerleaders. He found a website and had uniforms and colors picked out. He convinced the teacher that she should give them at least part of the morning each day to talk about and coordinate plays and for the girls to plan cheers…. I later found out she let them do because she was so impressed with how engaged and excited they were, so she made it a project! He told them the practices would be Wednesday nights at 6:00 p.m. in our yard. Kids were convinced this was real, went home and told their parents, which led to parents calling asking what time they should drop their kids off at my house. No joke.

Needless to say, people are naturally drawn to him and to what he has to say. He and I talk a lot about how special this gift is and the responsibility he has in owning it. My favorite part about him that stands out above everything else is how much he loves. He is selfless, empathetic, and empathic (more than he realizes), and sees things in others that they often do not see within themselves, and he doesn't hesitate to tell them so. He *loves* to talk and basically can talk to anyone about anything. He also tries to negotiate every. Single. Situation. He can talk himself out of any trouble he gets into just by working his charisma coupled with the way he can work words. He has talked himself out of homework, why his homework is late but he doesn't deserve it to be marked late, why they should have bouncy ball seats in school, why they should be able to eat on the bus on way home from field trips...it goes on and on. Needless to say, whatever his path is, he has the potential to be a powerful and influential leader who, if connected to his truth, can and will change the world.

So you see where I am going with this example of my son? Our natural gifts, the things we are drawn to, that we are naturally good at, are our calling, and when we follow our calling and live out our vocation, everything else is taken care of. Everything falls into place, including money, including what we need to not only survive, but to thrive. God is Love and Love is infinite, and with it comes an infinite amount of abundance. There is always more than enough to go around, and there is nothing in the world that our God wants for us but to tap into it and to call it our own. Society and the world does an incredible job of firing up our ego and presenting us with circumstances around what "we should" be doing, giving us a false sense of what abundance looks like if we work hard enough and long enough. Without connection to truth, our ego takes the bait, silences our soul, and hence we tend to search for "work" based on disconnection, fear, and a mindset of lack. And guess what we get? Fear. Disconnection. Work that is just that – work. Labor for money. And when you are disconnected and in this mindset, there just never seems to be enough of it, does there?

I find it oddly comforting and motivating to remember that this reality is temporary. It frees me. Time is ticking, so how am I spending it? What am I here to do? What are you here to do?

We are here to learn, grow, live, love, explore, but most importantly, to be who we are fully and completely without apology.

Choose to leave the rest to God.

You have to show up as who you are, in your life and at work. You just might be surprised at what that means for you. It may open up doors you never even knew existed, or you may find yourself standing outside of doors you wouldn't have considered knocking on. New ways of doing things will be revealed to you, making the improbable seem probable, and people you don't know will begin to show up to show you the way. Decide to do what you want to do, and then go do it, knowing it's waiting for you to arrive. Do the work to speak confidently about what it is you want to do, and trust this new voice and shape that is truly you.

Listen to your heart. Pray and seek guidance. Meditate. Journal. Do the work to piece it together, because it's all there. Decide what feels right, let go of what doesn't, and go for what does with everything you've got.

EXERCISE

Following your journaling exercise of gratitude and connection, as a means of reflection, think back to your childhood.

• What is something you loved to do as a child that you stopped doing?

• Why did you stop?

• What is something you feel drawn to now and wish you could do more of?

• Why do you feel you can't do more of that thing?

• What is something you can envision yourself doing effortlessly, regardless of how hard it might be?

Now meditate on it and journal on what you hear! You should be surprised to see what you write down...!

CHAPTER 9

LIVING YOUR TRUTH

"Truly I tell you, this poor widow has put in more than all those who are contributing to the treasury. For all of them have contributed out of their abundance; but she out of her poverty has put in everything she had..."
– Mark 12:43-44 (NIV)

I love the story of the poor widow in the Bible, and it is perfect to open this chapter because it captures the essence of the required skills that pull us through to abundance – action, surrender, and emptying.

Abundance is our birthright and is an inherent byproduct of choosing and intentionally fulfilling our purpose. It comes from connection, faith, truth, self-love, and using the gifts God has given us to live a purposeful life. However, when we decide to tap into and manifest the abundance available to us through God and our good works, they key is to remember that it not only matters what we do, but how we do it.

The first step is action. We've talked about this before, but it is worth revisiting. You have to understand that knowing what you want to do to fulfill your purpose is not enough. We have to agree to fulfilling it with all of your heart and soul. It's all or nothing. The good news is that action comes easily when you are fully connected, as we discussed in previous chapters. When you know you are aligned to a bigger plan and that plan is perfect, there is nothing to fear. Being afraid is still going to creep up but remember, that's exactly what courage is: being afraid and doing it anyway.

You also have to be patient and keep showing up no matter what, trusting and knowing with every beat of your heart and with every breath in your lungs that God is going to deliver. So much so that you consider it done, and in believing so, you have to act like so. If you believe your purpose is to start a non-profit, then get cracking, girl! You have to show up at non-profit events, meet with people who run non-profits, put yourself out there and expect to find your way. Expect to find the next person who is going to carry you forward, expect money to come out of nowhere, because you know you are divinely guided. You know what to do – be grateful for what you have and for where you are going, pray and meditate, journal what you hear, use your intuition, and keep moving forward. You have to keep your dream in motion, signaling to the universe you are aligned and ready to receive what God has in store for you.

When we live with purpose, we choose to do so because it fills up our hearts, not our pockets. We know in our bones that what we receive – the joy, happiness, and peace our soul has been aching for is to be found just by living it.

PURPOSEFUL LIVING
LOOKS LIKE THIS

I have a great example of a woman living out her purpose that I can share with you to illustrate this point. There is a woman I will call Linda who works the front desk of my daughter's middle school. She is a petite woman with deep, dark brown eyes whose demeanor brings instant calm. Whether you hear her voice on the phone or you see her face when you walk in the door, she has this ability to project that she sees you. She sees you are tired. She sees you are frustrated. She sees you are sad, and she is there to help.

Now, if you have a middle schooler or have raised a middle schooler, you can fully appreciate what I'm about to say. If not, know this – middle school is brutal right now. It's everything we remember it to be, awkward and awful, full of insecurity, hormones, acne, and the need for validation and acceptance, but now add in social media platforms like Snapchat and VSCO, where all those insecurities are readily displayed, called out, and violated. Drugs are more accessible than ever, and the heroin epidemic claims its victims every day, leading our children to live lives of addiction or loss due to overdose. Or their parents are active users themselves and have overdosed, leaving the world with a new group of orphaned adolescents with soaring rates of depression, anxiety, and risk of suicide. Not good.

Linda meets these children every morning and offers the gift of herself every day, completely and fully. She was just telling me that her youngest daughter just turned sixteen and she and her husband were talking about where their lives are heading now that they are close to being empty nesters. She said she recently was thinking about her life and how difficult this job can be on certain days. They were talking about her maybe considering a different job. She recalled how she was a successful businesswoman in sales at one time in her life. She said to me,

"I recently thought about going back to sales, but how could I? Would I make more money? Of course. Could I be incredibly successful at it because I connect so easily to and with other people? Yup. But I can't leave these children. Many times I am the only one who will ever ask them if they are OK, if they've eaten that day, if they have a place to go home to. They need me. I want to take each of them home with me to love them, but I know I cannot, so I do what I can with what I have and can do for them, and it fills me up."

Purpose. Linda is living her purpose. She isn't doing it for any other reason than the assurance that she is making a difference. Will someone recognize her for this someday? God, I hope so. But she doesn't care if that ever happens. That's not why she's there. She's not there to be recognized, she's there because her soul is alive while she's there. She is using her gifts and shining her light on the darkness in that school and lifting some of the burden from the children who walk through that door. She is there to be Love. The kind of love that these children and the world so desperately need right now. She's exactly where she is supposed to be. Most importantly, she recognized she has options that might be more lucrative, but she is wise enough to know that money is empty. It's only paper if there isn't love energy behind it, so what would that bring her? Not nearly the kind of personal reward and honor she feels by giving of herself so willingly and so freely.

SURRENDER AND EMPTYING: MOTHER TERESA AND GANDHI

St. Mother Teresa is one of my favorite saints of all time. I caught a glimpse of her once when, believe it or not, she visited my little hometown. It was quite a big to-do. She was well into her eighties when I saw her. I remember thinking how small and frail she looked, yet her presence was profound and drew quite a crowd. She was clearly incredibly powerful and, in my naivety, I remember thinking, "wow, how can a little nun who is so poor and so frail be so powerful?" She is a perfect example of someone who understood the power of going all in and what true surrender was all about.

I return often to reflect on what resonates with me the most about her story: she didn't set out on her mission to become what she became. She simply walked out her door and began with the first poor, homeless person lying in the gutter in the slum that she came across and she loved them. That's it. She didn't ask for followers. They came to her. She didn't seek out validation from anyone. She believed she was divinely guided. She believed she was fulfilling her purpose and in doing so, she didn't need to worry about anything other than serving.

She didn't seek out money or worry about where it would come from – she just believed that she would be taken care of completely in every possible way, and in turn, she magnetized abundance like a magic sorcerer. Even when she was offered money, she didn't just take it from anyone, in fact, there are a number of stories of how she would often turn large sums of gifted money away. In the book *No Greater Love*, we learn the story of a rich woman who came to Mother Teresa telling her she admired her work and wanted to help. When Mother Teresa asked her to identify a weakness, she admitted that she loved to buy and wear elegant saris and that most cost an average of 800 rupees. Mother Teresa's response on how she could help? She told her from now on to buy saris that are worth no more than 500 rupees and donate the rest to her charity. You see, she wasn't interested in the money just for the sake of money. She was interested in reaching and teaching the soul of the giver, uncovering and refining their intention for giving, and that was the real work to be offered up to God for which she was always rewarded. It is exactly why it was so hard to keep her poor.

Mother Teresa showed us not only what it looked like to surrender, but her life exemplifies the abundance that is given to us when we do.

Gandhi is another powerful example of surrender and emptying. Gandhi believed that the only way to change the world was to let God, or Soul Force as he called it, work through you, and in order to do that, you and your desires had to get out of the way. He called this "reducing yourself to zero," so God can do the work. It is the ultimate form of detachment and surrender. He once wrote, "There comes a time when an individual becomes irresistible and his actions become all-pervasive in its effects. This comes when he reduces himself to zero."

My "reduce me to zero" prayer is this: "May the work come to me, and may it be lived through me so abundance can do the same." I pray this prayer before every client meeting, with the intention for both of us to find our way. We know how this turned out for Gandhi and for Mother Teresa. They lived lives with incredible abundance, had immeasurable impact on the world and left a legacy that will live on forever.

God sees our deeds. He knows the contents of our hearts and our intentions. When we are truly doing our best to live out our purpose and doing so not caring about the outcome, we activate abundance, and with God, the return on investment is exponential. God delivers for on us in every way. He always will. As I said before, He will deliver in a way that you will not only survive, but you will thrive, and your soul and the fruits of your soul thriving will begin to manifest in our material lives.

Surrender, empty yourself, take action aligned to truth, and you become unstoppable.

I used to almost fear success and abundance because I felt guilty. I was proud of my success, but I always somehow felt guilty for having all the abundance I received from my hard work. Although it didn't seem right to have so much while others were suffering, I knew I wasn't Mother Teresa or Gandhi. I was a mother of two who was asking to understand how I could feel more fulfilled with my life. I knew God wasn't asking me to give away all of my family's money and literally become poor, but I knew there was something I was missing. Something I needed to do differently or think about differently. This was part of the invitation for me and really another prompt from my soul at the beginning of my journey here. Understanding what it meant to be poor in spirit, and how to surrender and empty myself allowed me to fully understand the extent of God's love, the energy model he put in place for us to access, how I could tap into it, and what I was expected to do with what I got out of it.

One Sunday in church, the priest told the congregation that we should think of God as our father and that He loves us the way we love our children. He went as far as to say that this was one of the gifts embedded in being a parent – that we have a deeper and richer understanding of the extent of God's love for us. When I think about my children, I know I would give up my life for them if it came down to me saving them from some serious suffering. Sound familiar?

When we love someone, we also love to see and make them happy, right? We love to see them light up when we give them something we know they are asking for or wanting. Think about when you are buying Christmas gifts for your kids or a special loved one. You want to give them everything they ask for and maybe a little something they don't even know they want until they have it. As parents, we don't want to just give them what they want, we want to surprise them and surpass their expectations.

Now make yourself God, we are His creation, His children who He looks lovingly upon in His infinite power and unconditional Love. When we ask for something, He wants to give it to us. He wants to wow us. If it is aligned to our gifts and purpose, is good for us, and we intend to use it for the good of not only ourselves, but the world, *we can have whatever we want, just by asking for it.* When we do, The Universe aligns itself to put it in front of you or delivers it to you for your taking with the expectation that it is to flow through us and back out into the world for the good of all. We simply become an outlet for Him to co-create with us, for great things to be created through us; things that, with His help, change the world for the better. When I came to understand this, the guilt, the fear of success that my ego created around money, around the abundance God gifted to me, dissolved right before my eyes when deciding to do this work. I have been blessed with tremendous abundance in my life and I know more is on the way. We already have a plan of how we are going to use it.

All of that being said, just like a mother or father of a young child, He also knows what is best for us. Just like we wouldn't give our five-year-old a knife to cut up his or her carrots even though the child believed he needed and wanted the knife, God sometimes protects us by not giving us what we want. Again, you can't fool him. He knows your heart better than you know yourself. We receive abundance only when our intentions are pure of heart.

So, what does this mean for you right now? Well, if you are entertaining the invitation to this journey, know you have everything you need to make the changes you need to make to live the life of our dreams, the one in your heart that is calling you, that your soul will show you, readily available to you. It's all there. What is it going to take to manifest it?

Connection. Transformation. Unconditional self-love. Trust. Belief. Gratitude. Surrender.

CHAPTER 10

FLOW AND RESISTANCE

*"If you bring forth what is within you, what you bring forth
will save you; if you do not bring forth what is within you, what
you do not bring forth will destroy you."*

– Gnostic Gospel of Thomas

I love *Star Wars*. I remember falling in love with the whole
concept of the series when my husband bought the box set of
the first six movies for my son. As a family, we binge-watched
them over a long weekend during a big snowstorm. By the end
of *Return of the Jedi*, I was hooked. Of course, I began to ana-
lyze everything that underpinned the movie – the Force, the
Jedi, the First Order, good, bad, everything in between. Now
that the hero of VIII and IX is female, I'm *really* over the moon.
Talk about women ruling the world. Rock on.

When I look back over the saga in totality, one story has
always stood out to me more than any other. That is the story
of Anakin Skywalker. His story epitomizes the constant battle
we fight every day, the battle of ego vs. true self.

For those reading this who do not know anything about *Star Wars*, let me break Anakin's story down for you. Anakin Skywalker was one of the most powerful Jedi who ever lived. The Jedi were considered the guardians of peace and justice. They were basically the good guys who were trained how to use the Force – an invisible power that connected all things – for good. Anakin was a smart, loving child who took care of his mother and was always helping others. He was raised as a slave on a planet called Tatooine, and his life changed when he, as a young child, agreed to enter a very dangerous pod race.

That day in the race, his natural abilities and connection with the Force were recognized and by an older Jedi. He ultimately left his home, was trained by a Jedi Knight named Obi-Wan Kenobi and grew into a very powerful Jedi who became very well aware of his powers, including the fact that they surpassed his mentors. He believed he was ready to take on and do more than he was being asked to. He quickly became proud and frustrated and believed he was being held back from reaching his true potential by Obi-Wan. Anakin ultimately becomes a Jedi Knight but remains unruly and reckless with his abilities, which is met with some serious side-eye by his peers.

He ultimately begins to seek counsel outside of the Jedi Knights, including from Chancellor Palpatine, who is a very powerful being on the dark side. His relationship with Palpatine causes Anakin some serious confusion and suffering. He is lost, so he begins to believe more and more of what Chancellor had to say, driving him further and further from the Jedi.

Out of fear and anger and frustration that now ruled his heart, Anakin submits and becomes Palpatine's apprentice on the dark side, and steps into his new power as Darth Vader, choosing to live contrary to his purpose.

Anakin's life reflects so many aspects of our reality. In his story, as a child he was freed from a life of slavery and given tremendous natural gifts which result in access to power and abundance, with the expectation of receiving it gracefully and using it wisely, of giving back to the world and making it better by doing the work to become a Jedi Knight.

We too have been saved from the slavery of confinement by being given free will to think and choose to do whatever we want. We have been born with gifts and access to innate superpowers to guide us on our journey leading us to a life of authentic happiness with the expectation that we receive it and let it flow through us, out into the world for the betterment of mankind.

But there is one pretty major kink in Anakin's character, isn't there? His ego is in the control room. We see so many aspects of ego-driving here – fear, pride, frustration, confusion leading to isolation, disillusionment, further confusion, attachment, seeking further power for his own sake, and ultimately darkness.

This is the path of ego.

In the movie, we see and hear his soul, the light, calling him and whispering to him, but he can't hear it because his ego is screaming and taunting him. It is a powerful force of nature, not to be feared, but to stay aware of. The more gifts we are given, the more power we have, the more our ego is built up and stands up, which only means we have more responsibility to be aware of its power, expect it to taunt us and be prepared for when it does, and know when we have to call on God to give us the strength to do the right thing. Being aware of the power of our ego has to be one of the driving forces for us to practice meditation daily and remain connected, because being connected allows us to not only reflect and course-correct, but to be able to understand that we have a choice. *We can choose flow.*

I have a bold ego who used to insist on driving. I thought that, because I was going to church and saying my prayers, I was connected. But in truth, I was living a life of ego. I often refused to ask for help and behaved in a way that sometimes isolated other people, especially at work where I believed few were working as hard as they should and certainly not as hard as me. I had high expectations for people, regardless of their circumstances.

At work, I was Anakin. I believed I was one of the best and deserved to be in a place of power. Although I was told over and over how talented I was and that I had a bright future, it wasn't good enough – how could they not see that I could do that job now? How could they not see I am ready? I don't need any further mentoring. "Just let me run with it," is what I would say, and when they'd say no, I would immediately be convinced they were not good leaders and couldn't recognize talent and gifts in others.

You hear it? You see it? Ego.

I work hard every day to balance the forces inside of me, and the way I do that best is by being aware of when my soul is out in front and when my ego comes out of the corner. I hear the difference in what I am thinking and what I am saying and how those thoughts create behavior.

As an example, let's pretend we are listening to a presentation about planning for an upcoming congress from a junior colleague outside of the field team.

My ego might say something like this to me: "You can do this better. This is not the direction we need to go."

To which I have learned to say, "You know what I see? Someone learning. We are learning too. Now, how can we love them into thinking differently about this situation to understand what they need to see so they can lead this team to where we need to go? Let's start thinking about that. Now go sit down."

This is much easier to do on a good day and much, much more difficult on a bad day.

But do you hear the difference in intention?

One sees the soul giving the talk. The other sees the opportunity for self-promotion.

One is more interested in the souls seeing each other and thriving together. The other is interested in what calling them out might get it.

One is interested in what is the best outcome for the team regardless of who gets the credit. The other is interested only in the credit for moving the team in the right direction.

Being cognizant of where and when your ego is likely to show up is the trick to keeping it reigned in, especially on a bad day. This takes us back to the need for gratitude meditation every morning. You should check in with how you are feeling when you wake, meditate, pray for help if needed, and then decide on how you are going to show up that day before your feet even hit the ground.

No one is perfect. We will fail. Our ego wins sometimes. No biggie. The trick is to forgive and love ourselves unconditionally. We do that by gentle self-reflection and creation of a plan for reparation – what have I learned from this? How can I recognize it next time? How can I make what I did right?

One of the other times ego tends to really beat us up is when challenges arrive in our life. It will invariably rear its ugly head in one shape or form, and with it, fear will show up *big time*. Fear makes it *so easy* to fall back into our old patterns, disconnecting us and inviting our ego to step in to try and come up with a solution. In fact, your ego will do its darnedest to convince you it knows the way. It's trying to protect you. It thinks it knows better. It's sly and rich in words and strong feelings that evoke strong emotions to sway us away from what we know as truth.

This is when we are likely tempted to choose resistance because we are uncomfortable, and uncomfortable feels bad.

We end up forgetting that our God always has a plan. When we resist the path God has put in front of us, we are sending a signal out into the universe that we don't need God's help. Remember, you have been given tremendous power, and we tap into that infinite energy field surrounding us just by thinking thoughts or speaking the words. Then the Universe aligns with whatever you say you need, including if you declare you want to be left alone, naturally attracting more fear and what we don't want.

We cannot do anything better than what God can and wants to do for us. He always has our backs and the trick to choosing flow is to approach our lives with the kind of surrender that exists within the heart of a child. *The kind of trust that surpasses hope.*

In a meditation about what this kind of trust looks like for us on earth, I was guided to think of a hungry newborn baby resting comfortably in its mothers' arms. The baby cries out to eat, but never doubts that his mother's breast is nearby and that it holds the milk that was created just for him, the milk that is always perfect in every way – in content, temperature, smell, and taste, continuously and endlessly made as is needed, even as he sleeps. This is the trust we are asked to have in unconditional Love.

Think about how the milk is made perfectly for the baby by his mothers body, who delivers it selflessly over and over again with so much love that, sometimes, her own pain is part of delivering it. She makes her raw nipples available at will because she knows that it is through the pain that there is nourishment and contentment and rest and growth. This is just like the life you have been given and the vocation you are intended to fill was created only for you. It was created perfect in every way, and our God serves it up to us with so much love that, sometimes, it is in the pain and suffering where the nourishment, growth, and needed rest in preparation for the path are delivered.

Just as the baby doesn't worry if he is going to miss a feeding, there is no reason for you to worry that you might miss what is intended for you. *Because no one else is you, and only you have been given the gifts necessary to navigate this beautiful, unique path to fulfillment that serves you and the world.*

So let go. Choose flow.

Flow with whatever life sends your way and, like a child, expect to be seen through it knowing your protector is The Universe. See every day as a gift regardless of what it holds. Approach your life and its joys, pains, ups and downs, celebrations and sufferings with newborn child-like trust, expecting that all of your needs will be met, and knowing that all of your suffering is with purpose, because you are loved.

Unconditionally loved.

And everything is going to be OK.

CHAPTER 11

CHALLENGES TO EXPECT

J oseph Campbell once labeled spiritual growth as the "hero's journey," with good reason.

If I told you that this journey was easy and that it was experienced the same way for everyone, that would be a blatant lie. Nothing that is worth doing is ever easy. You already know this. All of this is tough stuff, and it takes commitment and resilience. I promise you, it will be very easy to finish this book, put it down, and say, "Well, *that is good to know*," and never do anything with it. I get it. There are so many easier ways out and so many distractions pulling on us, calling for our attention, promising that if you just do this or get to that, it will magically help you live with more passion and have more happiness. You know now that you don't need something *better*. What you need is transformation and vocation.

Because of the level of disconnection today, I think one of the hardest parts of all this is recognizing the invitation and understanding what it really means. So many people fall into this cycle of feeling unfulfilled, thinking that working harder to get more of what they think they need will make them happy when nothing can be further from the truth. Longer hours, buying more, and doing more to try to fill the void is never going to be the answer, but many people just do not and will not see any other way. It's OK, and it's part of the process for many, but *they will keep coming up empty.*

The concern is that, over time, emptiness will start to degrade our values and morals, and we are led right down the path to the dark side, seeking more power and more control, thinking it is going to make us happy. Unfortunately, like Anakin, we end up losing who we are entirely and become someone we aren't really proud to be. Forgiveness is organically built into unconditional Love, but it is the suffering in between that can inflict deep wounds within us that change who we are emotionally and psychologically. The work becomes challenging in a different way, requiring of us more time and more resources to complete our journey. This isn't the end of the world by any means, but why make it more difficult?

I am not naive enough to think that the epidemic of disconnection is a problem that will be easily solved by introducing more spirituality alone, but it is one that we have to be aware of and work at to keep chipping away. The statistics blow my mind – we live in a world where depression and anxiety are more common than ever before in the history of the world. I have found that many people who are on this journey get stuck in transformation because they have a hard time transmuting pain from a deep wound caused by some type of trauma that was buried deep in the subconscious that your soul gently places in front of you during this process. This has the potential to impact every aspect of the journey forward so it must be managed carefully. It may even require additional counseling and other professional help. However, in general, overcoming the fear of what you may uncover and how to connect once you meet with your soul when you do is where a spiritual life coach can be a wonderful guide. When that wound is addressed, loved, and healed, it is life changing, but can also lead to people experiencing what feels like a very intense awakening. Awareness here is key, and again, where having a coach to love you through it can be critical to keep you on track. As we talked about in the beginning, finding and knowing and understanding self-love is tricky business, but it is the most important part of this journey since knowing you are worthy of unconditional Love is part of the foundation for spirit-mind-body wellness.

I can see how successful women, especially in the corporate world, can so easily be swayed into thinking that what they have to do is work harder, take a different angle, work on personal development, sharpen our influence skills, build our sponsors, or build a better, more marketable personal brand. Hard work is always part of the answer, just not the kind of work we think. I believe what women have the opportunity to do is to lead from our hearts and be brave enough to own that kind of leadership, showing the world what it can look like when our souls are connected and lead the way.

Remember Linda? Let's go back to visit with her again for a minute. There is something that Linda said that highlights this and another really important point that is worthy of exploring. She hinted that her siblings felt her to be inferior to them because of her job in sales. From what she said and how she said it, I felt that somehow, she felt that she wasn't good enough or worthy enough or doing good for the world since she was not as "smart" as her siblings. The truth is that Linda feeling she is "not as smart" as her siblings is completely irrelevant. Linda being attracted to sales and not engineering only means that Linda was blessed with different gifts. She may not have done as good in school as her sister, but I would place a strong bet her sister would never be able to connect to other people and sell them anything the way that Linda could. In this process of discerning purpose, we often come face-to-face with this demon derived from ego who tells us our purpose is not good enough or making a big enough impact, so it can't be our *real* purpose. There has to be more to it, right?

Nope. This is called *devaluing*, and the other end of the spectrum is *grandiosity*, as Stephen Cope describes beautifully in his book *The Great Work of Your Life*. We expect our purpose to be something that makes us feel we stand out and are recognized, but many times, when we look at our life and what we love to do, we might question what "living *that* purpose" would really mean to the world. We may feel like it's nothing more than a hill of beans, so why bother?

This is where grandiosity and devaluing collide, and the answer, as Stephen describes, is thinking of *the small as big.* We underestimate the weight we pull in this world just by being us and how every choice we make directly impacts every life around us. The truth is that our purpose may never be given an award or put on a grand stage and celebrated, but we have to remember that we are all connected, completely and fully, and everything we do impacts someone or something. We are all-powerful beings regardless of our earthly status, and we all are responsible for how we wield that power. One of my favorite teachings from the *Bhagavad Gita* of the Hindu tradition revolves around the mystic relationship of the individual to the universal. It is the story of Indra's Net.

Indra was known as the "thunderbolt god" who lived in the clouds at the peak of Mount Meru, which is the most sacred mountain of Hindu faith. Indra threw out a vast net of life over the mountain, stretching infinitely in all directions. Each "eye" where the net came together was held together by a glittering jewel.

Author Alan Watts, who was known for his ability to elegantly translate and describe eastern philosophy for western cultures, describes Indra's net this way:

"Imagine a multidimensional spider's web in the early morning covered with dewdrops. And every dewdrop contains the reflection of all the other dew drops. And, in each reflected dewdrop, the reflections of all the other dew drops in that reflection. And so ad infinitum."

What does it mean? Each jewel in the net is an individual soul which is itself, but simultaneously reflects and represents the entire net of souls. A change in the reflection of one jewel changes the reflection of the entire net. Therefore, each jewel holds the entire net within it.

This beautiful story represents the complexity and intricacy of our interconnectedness. We are individuals, yet we are all one, and within us, we hold the world. What we do, what we don't do, and how we do it impacts all of us. Big or small holds equal importance because each jewel is both simultaneously. Ultimately, the integrity of the net depends on each which impacts the whole. Each jewel, therefore, is called to do only one thing – be its utter true self, beaming and reflecting its light as much as possible, because as it does, each and every other jewel shines and shimmers too.

This should not intimidate you – hopefully, it should only draw you closer to the beauty and sacredness of this calling and process. Understand that the cost of resistance to God's plan for your life might be blocking you from living a life greater than you can imagine and by not living it, you are basically holding back the world. Choose flow. Choose trust. Choose the ultimate act of self-love and take the journey to become the you whose purpose in this reality completes the whole. The world is literally relying upon you to pull it through. This is a lot for our little minds and hearts to take on alone, and it can feel very overwhelming, which is why we have to remember we are never alone. We just have to connect and choose courage to step into the power of spirit-mind-body wellness, the power of who we are and what we are here to do, knowing and trusting that everything else is and will always be taken care of.

CHAPTER 12

WHAT SETS YOUR SOUL ON FIRE SETS YOUR LIFE ON FIRE AND CHANGES THE WORLD

"This being human is a guest house.
Every morning a new arrival.
A joy, a depression, a meanness,
some momentary awareness comes
as an unexpected visitor.
Welcome and entertain them all!
Even if they are a crowd of sorrows,
who violently sweep your house
empty of its furniture,
still, treat each guest honorably.
He may be clearing you out
for some new delight.
The dark thought, the shame, the malice.
meet them at the door laughing and invite them in.
Be grateful for whatever comes.
because each has been sent
as a guide from beyond."
— Jalal ad-Din Rumi

H ave I mentioned that my husband Mike and I are high school sweethearts? We've been together since high school, when I was a junior and he was a sophomore. Crazy, right? We both grew up in our little town. We both know it's a long time, and we talk about it often, especially around the holidays. But seeing how long it's been was another experience. Here is what I mean.

Over the Thanksgiving holiday, my sister found some old movies that my mom and dad recorded, mostly of Christmas mornings and sports events or theater performances. In March of 1993, there was a snowstorm in Northeastern Pennsylvania that dropped sixteen inches of snow. My sister found a video my mom made of that snowstorm and within it was a clip of Mike and I laying around that lazy snow day together. We were sixteen years old.

Now forty-three and forty-two, my eyes were opened to how young and innocent we were, how we were doing nothing but enjoying being together on a day off of school, flowing, and just happy to be alive. We have literally grown up together and staying married meant we had to choose to transform over and over together and learn to love each other over and over again. He was and still is my best friend. My parents were still together then, before things went south, so it was interesting to watch my mother's reaction too. I could feel from her the mixed emotions – the joy of the sweet memories of her family together, being younger, healthier, happier maybe, and having no idea what was about to come her way and how life is unpredictable. Yet there she sat and so did Mike and I alongside her, in this future state, enjoying time together, another Thanksgiving, another coming snowstorm.

Tick tock … time keeps on ticking, doesn't it?

Did you know that the average life span of the butterfly after its emergence from the cocoon is *one month*? Seems like such a short amount of time after all that transformation work, but time is relative, isn't it? It may be cliché, but as the old saying goes, maybe it's not so much how much time we have, but rather what we do with it. In this precious time we are given, how do we live fully? How do we live with authentic happiness and presence, taking in the magic of the life we have been given? What's the secret sauce?

I think my husband captured it quite elegantly in a Mother's Day gift he gave me. I keep it in my drawer and return to it now and again, especially now having a teenager and being a year away from having two. I guess I'm going to have to laminate it.

In this card, he writes how much he and the kids love me, how much they look up to me, how much they admire my strength, grit, grind, and passion for life, and how much of it influences him and our children every day. He shared how parenting our children is such a difficult but joyous journey and how the work it takes to be good parents doesn't feel so hard when we do it together. He talks about how he loves that we are never afraid to put the hard stuff on the table and dig into it, and how we all show up to those discussions just as we are and with what we are feeling – angry, frustrated, loud, passionate – as well as how we feel permission to show up this way because we know we can, because we know it's real. We also know we always figure things out and when we do it together, we do it better and faster. Most importantly, perhaps, the creating of that safe and sacred space is our doing and we should acknowledge it.

As a mother and a wife, I was reminded of the privilege I have to do what I do and that what I do and say, as well as how I do it – parenting, loving, failing, getting back up and teaching by example – all only means showing up every time, all the time, just as we are, because we are all learning together. Right now, we are learning how to control anger and frustration, quiet our minds, and the power of unashamedly sharing what is in our hearts, even when it's hard to do so. We are learning alongside of our growing children and our aging bodies. We constantly try, fail, forgive, get back up, and try again and again and again, loving each other through it all.

What I realized is that this is the secret sauce of work and life – *all of it* – knowing and appreciating the grit, grind, frustration, anger, suffering, pain, forgiveness, learning, growing, and subsequent joy that eventually stems from it all is what makes life worth living.

It is exactly how we give each other the courage to seek our true selves and to live true authenticity, allowing us to build up the courage to show up as who we really are outside of our sacred space. This, in turn, results in seeking opportunities that naturally lead us to true happiness because we already understand what it truly feels like to be alive.

It is being aware that it is in the ordinary, the everyday, where our purpose is always being re-invented. We are dynamic beings connected to a dynamic world, full of the awe, wonder, and energy of life. The journey to connecting to that energy and flowing with it is exactly in those moments where our true purpose is unearthed over and over again. It is where the gift of true happiness lies.

Our job is to remain open to experiencing everything that life throws at us – the joy, happiness, and exhilaration of earned success, but also the pain, suffering, agony, and struggle that will fill many of our days and nights. We have to welcome it all and most importantly, give up trying to understand it. The gift of unknowing has to be integrated into our hearts, but it is in the unknowing and uncertainty where faith is tested, strengthened, and grown. It is in these experiences where the real soul of life lies, where our hearts call to us and show us the truth over and over again. If we listen intently and surrender fully, lessons are learned, and we begin to understand that life is so much more than seeking material things that will never make us happy.

We have to choose to be present and show up every day so in love with who we know we are and everything we know we aren't, then still be brave enough to go all-in –because that's when life gets interesting.

We begin to understand that it's often the pain of life that gives us what we need to do the next thing, including experiencing a different level of happiness and different kind of fulfillment – the kind that does not turn up empty, leading us to want, wish, and work for more – but the kind that fills us up in a different way. So we have to keep showing up, especially when it's really hard to do because we know it ultimately allows us to reap strength, authentic connection to ourselves and others, and exponential growth, all of which allows us to emerge confident, new, and whole.

At some point, we will get the opportunity to look back on our lives and have this moment of total clarity where we will get to see the big picture. We will finally fully and completely understand the paradox of the experience as a whole. I believe we will see that the pain, the suffering, and all the agony was worth every single minute. We will understand it had purpose.

And we will say that we would do it all again in a heartbeat.

The most beautiful gift will be confirmation that, all along, we were indeed carried and guided, and everything, *everything*, was perfect and given to us in perfect timing.

This is why I am so passionate about being connected and want to show people how to fall in love with life and with the God who created it all – so that we all can wake up every day and know there can be no other way. We can begin to create heaven here on earth. Each day we can choose to believe we are unconditionally loved, and it will all work out in the end, because one day it will all make sense. For now, all we are asked to do is love so well that it lights up our days so we can light up the world and the way for others who need the light. Our actions derived from purposeful living connect us to and ultimately create the world we see and know. Big or small, the power our actions hold is beyond our understanding, and we have to own the responsibility, nonetheless, recognizing the Anakin inside of us, knowing that we hold the power to influence, create, and destroy the inner order of the Universe.

I wrote this book to help guide you to your vocation in order to live that passionate life you are seeking, because I believe by doing so, we fulfill our sacred duty to be our truest, shiniest gem in our corner of the net, bringing out the light in others to do the same, which will change the world. If each individual soul doesn't transform to find its vocation and live out its purpose, our egos will continue to rule the world and we will continue with the "I" project, and time is very good at reminding us where that project is going. Do we not see it happening? Every day we are alive, we are dying simultaneously, and in the end, that project of "I" is going right to the grave.

When we seek vocation and live with purpose to serve, fears of death dissipate because we don't have time to think about our death – we are too caught up in being alive. We don't care if we succeed or fail. We just know we are fulfilled, loved, and connected to ourselves and something bigger than ourselves.

Regardless of where you are right now, in work or in your life, whether it is in a season of joy or a season of pain, choose to acknowledge it and choose to let it all in. Welcome it with open arms. Celebrate, trust, pray, and allow your soul to be filled with resilient hope and peace. Be so grateful for your life and blessings that there is no room for anything other than Love. Choose to show up to the people in your life and commit to loving each other relentlessly through the mess of your time here in Pandora, knowing and believing that connection to Love is all you need. Believe that everything is exactly as it should be. You are loved unconditionally, and everything is going to be more than OK. It is going to be amazing.

I will leave you with the wise words young Emma wrote in her page in the *Book of Days*:

"Believe me future Wildflower:
You are living an extraordinary life,
Day by glorious day.
Never doubt your starry aim."

– Natalie Lloyd

ACKNOWLEDGMENTS

This book is a dream of mine that came to reality with the guidance and help of many entities, human and spirit.

Michael – there is no one who knows me, sees me, and loves me the way you do. I know that I would not be who I am today without the foundation of who we are, yet you've always let me dream. When I decided to chase my dreams, you let me soar, even when soaring meant days and nights at my computer without a shower while you managed our messy, beautiful life. All you are, all you bring to me and our family, and what you've allowed me to bring to this book is more than acknowledged – it is honored. I have loved you for lifetimes. You are, always will be, and always have been my soulmate.

Anna Mary and Michael Joseph, thank you for choosing me to be your mom. Thank you for acknowledging that I am doing the best that I can and loving me anyway. You both have taught me more than you know. I love you both more than there are words to express; you are my heart living outside of my body. I pray I can teach you the concepts in this book not by preaching them, but by living them so that you know you can too.

Mom and Tricia, we've come a long way, baby! Thank you for always seeing me and believing in me. I couldn't have done this without your encouragement, love, and constant force of positivity, even when it was really hard for all of us. I love you.

Angela Lauria, I prayed for you and you showed up in a way bigger than I ever could have imagined. I am beyond grateful to know you, work with you, and learn from you. This world we are creating is going to be exactly as we dream it to be. I can't wait to see where it takes all of us next. So much honor and love to you, your work, your passion, and your vision.

My Quill family, you loved me through my transformation – now let us love each other and our fellow human avatars through theirs. It is our time.

Andrae and Emily, thank you for sharing your gifts with me and for your wise and excellent counsel. You pushed me forward. Thank you for helping me to make this book everything I hope it will be.

To all my extended family and friends who are family, thank you for all of your love and encouragement throughout the writing of this book. You know who you are. I love you.

THANK YOU

Thank you for reading *Your Time Is Now: The Roadmap to Finding Your Passion and the Courage to Pursue It*. I hope you enjoyed it and I hope it has made an impact on your life in some way. As a bonus gift, I have recorded a special video masterclass for you that serves as an adjunct to this book. Please email me at soulfuel23@gmail.com for the link to your bonus gift!

ABOUT THE AUTHOR

T ammy L. Breznitsky is a specialty trained infectious diseases Doctor of Pharmacy who launched Soul2Soul Transformations, LLC to answer the call in her heart to serve others in a new way. Over the past fourteen years, Tammy has dedicated her life to supporting patients and working with communities of researchers developing medicines for the treatment of Hepatitis C, HIV, and Non-Alcoholic Steatohepatitis (NASH). The culmination of time and experience in this work unveiled an unmet need of people worldwide.

This background, coupled with her passion to bring others to know the God who carried her through life with a mentally and physically abusive father, inspired her to pursue her new purpose: helping people understand the importance of connection with a higher power and how this connection with God is key to unlocking and knowing true self, which ultimately fuels unconditional self-love and serves as the catalyst to resilient transformation. Her life-long love of fitness and passion for teaching others how to implement and live a sustainable and practical healthy lifestyle completes the mind-body-spirit triad on which her holistic wellness and spiritual life coaching business, Soul2Soul Transformations, is based.

ABOUT DIFFERENCE PRESS

Difference Press is the exclusive publishing arm of The Author Incubator, an educational company for entrepreneurs – including life coaches, healers, consultants, and community leaders – looking for a comprehensive solution to get their books written, published, and promoted. Its founder, Dr. Angela Lauria, has been bringing to life the literary ventures of hundreds of authors–in–transformation since 1994.

A boutique–style self–publishing service for clients of The Author Incubator, Difference Press boasts a fair and easy–to–understand profit structure, low–priced author copies, and author–friendly contract terms. Most importantly, all of our #incubatedauthors maintain ownership of their copyright at all times.

LET'S START A MOVEMENT WITH YOUR MESSAGE

In a market where hundreds of thousands of books are published every year and are never heard from again, The Author Incubator is different. Not only do all Difference Press books reach Amazon bestseller status, but all of our authors are actively changing lives and making a difference.

Since launching in 2013, we've served over 500 authors who came to us with an idea for a book and were able to write it and get it self–published in less than 6 months. In addition, more than 100 of those books were picked up by traditional publishers and are now available in book stores. We do this by selecting the highest quality and highest potential applicants for our future programs.

Our program doesn't only teach you how to write a book – our team of coaches, developmental editors, copy editors, art directors, and marketing experts incubate you from having a book idea to being a published, bestselling author, ensuring that the book you create can actually make a difference in the world. Then we give you the training you need to use your book to make the difference in the world, or to create a business out of serving your readers.

ARE YOU READY TO MAKE A DIFFERENCE?

You've seen other people make a difference with a book. Now it's your turn. If you are ready to stop watching and start taking massive action, go to http://theauthorincubator.com/apply/.

"Yes, I'm ready!"

DIFFERENCE
P R E S S

OTHER BOOKS BY DIFFERENCE PRESS

So, You Want to Be a Superintendent?: Become the Leader You Were Meant to Be by Donna Marie Cozine Ed.D.

Outsmart Endometriosis: Relieve Your Symptoms and Get Your Career Back on Track by Jessica Drummond DNC, CNS, PT

Teach and Go Home: The Sophisticated Guide to Simplifying and Managing Your Workload and More by Danielle E. Felton

The Wealthy Entrepreneur: The Formula for Making Money and Gaining Financial Clarity in Your Business by Robert Gauvreau FCPA

TMJ Is Ruining My Life: Managing Jaw Pain so You Can Eat Normally by Chelsea Liebowitz PharmD, MSCR

My Child's Not Depressed Anymore: Treatment Strategies That Will Launch Your College Student to Academic and Personal Success by Melissa Lopez Larson M.D.

The 9 Pillars of the YONIVERSE: Attract Amazing Clients as a Female Tantric Practitioner by Palki Mawar

Evolved NLP: The Impact-Driven Coach's Guide to Amplified Revenue and Results by Laura Slinn, Kelley Oswin RSW, and Ernie Pavan

Death Is Not Goodbye: Connect with Your Loved Ones Again by Kim Weaver

The Happy, Healthy Revolution: The Working Parent's Guide to Achieve Wellness as a Family Unit by Theresa Wee M.D.

Reprogram Your Sleep: The Sleep Recipe that Works by Tara Youngblood